SECRETS ABOUT MEN EVERY WOMAN SHOULD KNOW

▼▼▼▼▼▼▼▼▼▼▼▼▼▼▼▼▼▼▼▼▼▼▼▼▼▼

SECRETS ABOUT

MEN

EVERY WOMAN SHOULD KNOW

▲▲▲▲▲▲▲▲▲▲▲▲▲▲▲▲▲▲▲▲▲▲▲▲▲▲

Barbara De Angelis, Ph.D.

Delacorte Press

Published by
Delacorte Press
Bantam Doubleday Dell Publishing Group, Inc.
666 Fifth Avenue
New York, New York 10103

Library of Congress Cataloging in Publication Data

De Angelis, Barbara.
  Secrets about men every woman should know / by Barbara De Angelis.
    p.   cm.
  ISBN 0-385-29961-3
  1. Men—Psychology.   2. Masculinity (Psychology).   3. Sex
differences (Psychology).   4. Men—Sexual behavior.   5. Interpersonal
relations.   I. Title.
HQ1090.D4   1990
155.6'32—dc20   89-17239
                                                                        CIP

Manufactured in the United States of America
Published simultaneously in Canada

February 1990
BVG   10 9 8 7 6 5 4 3 2

TO JEFFREY

for teaching me that I don't have to chase
after love anymore

ACKNOWLEDGMENTS

I want to express my gratitude to the following people:

My family, for loving me unconditionally, always believing in me, and helping me get through a very difficult year of my life.

My fellow adventurers—Jamie Branker, Kevin Roesch, and Jeffrey James, for giving me the courage to look at the truth regardless of the outcome, for taking the leap with me, for building a bridge of love to help me make it to the other side.

Bill Chappelle, for showing up again in my life at just the right time, for sharing my vision and standing by my side, both as my friend and as the director of the Los Angeles Personal Growth Center.

David Sams, my business partner and manager, for helping me make my dreams come true, and especially for knowing that this book needed to be written.

Heather Simbrow Baroff, for her loyalty, her consistent good work in managing my office, and her wonderful presence.

Virginia Bussinger, my personal assistant, for her invaluable help in making my life work and keeping me organized.

Lisa Guyer, for taking such good care of me and my home while I was writing this book.

Maria Talamini, for driving me to CNN for two years, and for silently holding my hand when I needed it.

The entire assistants team and support team of Making Love Work seminars, for being the wind beneath my wings.

Bill Gannon and #804 at Polo Beach Club on Maui, for the perfect place to write.

George Oliva and Bill Lewis of KFI Radio in Los Angeles, for giving me a way to help so many people every day.

Bob Miller, editor in chief at Delacorte, for trusting me to know what's right, and for being so much fun to work with.

Harvey Klinger, my fabulous literary agent, for the best deals and most entertaining phone calls an author could want.

Ron Scolastico and The Guides, and William Rainen and Dr. Peebles, for their continuing wisdom and direction, and for always being there just when I need them most.

Rabbi David Baron, for being the voice of truth and a light in the darkness, my teacher, my brother, my friend.

Verne Varona, for everything—the love and the heartache—without which I couldn't have written this book.

And especially, and again, Jeffrey James, for being my rock, for patiently loving me out of my pain, for bringing stability into my life and peace into my heart.

CONTENTS

SECRETS ABOUT MEN AND WOMEN TOGETHER

SECRETS
ABOUT
MEN
EVERY
WOMAN
SHOULD
KNOW

INTRODUCTION

Have you ever wished that men would come with instruction booklets? If you buy a toaster, or an answering machine, it's always accompanied by a nice little booklet that helps you understand the product, explains it's features, and tells you how to avoid hurting yourself when you use it. Well, what about men? As women, we "use" men more than our other "appliances," yet we're expected to figure out how they work all by ourselves.

Every day of our lives, you and I deal with men—our husbands or boyfriends, our bosses or employers, our fathers, our sons, our friends. We try to understand them, to take care of them, to communicate with them, to love them—and to get them to love us back. When it works, we think men are fantastic, and we're sure we couldn't live without them. When it doesn't work, we think men are impossible, and that we'd be much better off never having to deal with them at all. If you're like me, I'm sure that at some point in your life you've thrown your hands up in frustration and felt like saying, "Send this man back to the factory—he's defective! There must be a part missing, because he sure isn't functioning properly," or, "Maybe this model has been discontinued—I can't make him work right!"

As a woman, you have three choices as to how you are going to deal with men during your lifetime:

Choice #1: You can get angry at the men in your life for driving you crazy and spend your time complaining about them. (This is fun for a few hours, but after a few years, it loses its attraction.)

Choice #2: You can give up men entirely and buy a nice, fluffy dog. (This is cheaper, and less work, but not very fulfilling.)

Choice #3: You can decide to learn everything there is to know about understanding and getting along with men, so that you can have the wonderful relationships you deserve.

I've spent the past fifteen years working with tens of thousands of men and women, learning about what makes relationships succeed and what makes them fail. It's taken me a long time to understand men. It's been a difficult and often painful journey—and I've made a lot of mistakes along the way in my own relationships with men.

I'm happy to say that not only have I survived, I've emerged from my struggle with a new understanding of men that has changed my life, and I want to share the things I've learned with you. I hope *Secrets About Men Every Woman Should Know* will be the instruction manual about men that you've been looking for. May it help you create the loving relationship with a man that you've always dreamed of.

ECRETS

ABOUT HOW WOMEN RELATE TO MEN

1 | Men: The Final Frontier

May you live in changing times.

—Chinese curse

I magine for a moment that you've been chosen to be part of an expedition to another planet. All that's known about the planet is that it is inhabited by beings whose physical appearance is similar to yours. After a long journey through space, you arrive at this faraway world. You step out of your spaceship and are greeted by pleasant-looking creatures who do indeed closely resemble your own species. Much to your amazement, they even appear to be speaking English.

Over the next few hours, you attempt to talk and interact with these beings. At first, you seem to be getting along well. But as more time passes, the tension between you and them begins to mount. Even though these aliens seem to understand the English language, they constantly misunderstand your attempts to communicate with them—you say one thing, and they hear another; you try to express curiosity, for instance, and they interpret it as criticism. As you observe these beings interacting with one another, the differences between you and them become even more apparent. Your

3

own species has been trained to value cooperation and emotional sensitivity—these beings seem always to be in competition with each other. You've been taught to share your feelings—they seem to work hard at hiding theirs. The more time you spend with these unusual creatures, the more frustrated you become.

Finally, you and your exploration team decide to depart from this strange and unsettling place. You're certain that these beings will be happy to see you go, since they didn't show much enthusiasm toward you during your visit. But to your great surprise, they become very sad when you announce that you are leaving, insist that they loved the time they spent with you, and beg you not to depart. In spite of their protests, you board your spaceship, more confused than ever. And as you settle back into your seat and feel the rocket engines lift the steel craft back into space, you think to yourself, *That was the strangest group of people I've ever met. They said one thing and felt another. They acted like they didn't care, but they did. They didn't seem to enjoy having us around, but were unhappy when we left. Well, they were interesting to visit, but I sure wouldn't want to live with them.*

Starting Your Adventure into the World of Men

Well, in case you haven't figured it out yet, the aliens have landed and are living among us—they're called "men." And when you consider the tremendous biological, psychological, and sociological differences between us, men might as well be from another planet. Stop and think for a minute about the odds of your getting along with someone who came from a very different background, was brought up with completely different values, and was taught to think, behave, and communicate in a totally different style from your own. Next to impossible, right? Yet every day of our lives, we attempt to challenge these odds by having relationships with men. The truth is, it's a miracle that we get along at all!

The differences between men and women have existed throughout the ages, as I explain in the remainder of this chapter. For thousands of years, women accepted these differences, adapted to them, and took on certain roles that were expected of us. But sometime around the beginning of the twentieth century a revolution took place, a revolution in the way women saw themselves and insisted on being seen by men. For the first time, women were demanding equality in all aspects of life, and in the process, were breaking out of those culturally stereotyped roles they and their mothers and their grandmothers and their great-grandmothers had complacently accepted. The later introduction of effective birth control methods and the flow of women into the work force gave women reproductive and economic freedom from dependance on men.

And so, a crisis in male-female relationships was born. Men were used to being in control, and expected women to behave submissively. Now women were saying, "No, I don't want to act that way anymore." The truth was that we still weren't sure of how we were supposed to act as "new women." We were confused, and our confusion made the men in our lives even more perplexed. It's as if we were still playing the same game, but all the old rules were thrown out, and we hadn't finished making up the new ones yet. One minute we wanted to be liberated; the next, we wanted to be taken care of. We went to work and learned to support ourselves, but we still expected a man to hold the door for us on the way into our office. We begged men to open up and show us their vulnerabilities, but found ourselves getting turned off when they started sounding weak. And while our own double standards bothered us, they drove men crazy.

As women of the 1990s, we are on the way to mastering our professional and financial lives. But when it comes to our relationships with men, we're more frustrated than ever, and sometimes it seems as if we haven't made any progress at all. As one very successful female business executive said to me recently, "I can figure out how to make my company hundreds of thousands of dollars and how to buy my own condominium, but I still can't figure out how to have a good relationship with a man!" For this woman, as well as for many of us, men are the "final frontier," the one area that remains an untamed mystery in our lives.

▼

Warning: This is *not* a "men are jerks" book! It isn't about blaming men, or making them wrong for how they behave

▲

INSTEAD, IT'S A COLLECTION OF VALUABLE INFOR-MATION THAT I'VE SHARED WITH THOUSANDS OF WOMEN, INFORMATION THAT HAS HELPED THEM UNDER-STAND WHY MEN ARE THE WAY THEY ARE, AND TAUGHT THEM NEW WAYS TO RELATE TO MEN.

Why Men Are the Way They Are

Have you ever wondered why men prefer to drive around lost for hours rather than stop and ask for directions?

Have you ever suspected that the men who try to control you are secretly afraid of the power you have over them?

Have you ever wondered why men have such a hard time letting you get really close to them?

Have you ever wondered why men get so upset when they are trying to concentrate on something and you try to get them to pay attention to you?

Have you ever asked yourself why a man will insist he isn't worried or upset when you absolutely know he is?

If you answered yes to any of the above questions, you aren't alone. Every woman knows the frustration of looking at the man she loves and feeling like she cannot understand why he is the way he is. The first thing you need to know is:

▼

Men aren't the way they are because they want to drive women crazy; they've been trained to be that way for thousands of years. And that training makes it very difficult for men to be intimate

---
▲

Here, then, is some background information. Let's look at:

1. Why I Call Men "The Solitary Hunter" and "The Displaced Warrior"
2. Why Men Have Always Dominated Women
3. How Men Are Trained to Be Unfit for Love
4. How TV Teaches Us Stereotyped Sex Roles

Man: The Solitary Hunter

The time is thousands of years ago. The earth is an often violent, changing planet complete with volcanos, ice storms, floods, and harsh extremes of climate. Wild animals roam freely, far outnumbering the still-meager population of human beings, who live in small groupings whenever they can find shelter. The world is a primitive place, where survival of the fittest is the only reality.

Huddled inside a cave on a hillside, a family eats their one meal of the day—the last few scraps of meat from a wild deer killed by the male two days before. The meat is all that is left from that hunt. The male has tried unsuccessfully to find more food, but hunting is difficult in this weather. It's been snowing for a week, and most of the animals have left and gone south to warmer valleys. But as he watches his woman and their two small children greedily lick every morsel from their fingers, he knows what he must do—he must go out and hunt, and he must not come back until he has killed. If he fails, he and his family will die, and will be eaten themselves by the wolves he hears howling every night.

Suddenly, the male leaps toward the entrance to the cave, his body poised for attack—he thinks he hears a suspicious sound. Perhaps it is another, more powerful male, hoping to kill him and take his woman and the cave for his own. Or perhaps it is a wolf or a lion, ready to attack and satisfy its hunger. Or perhaps it is just the wind; he cannot be sure. He is never sure. That is why he will not sit with his back toward the cave opening, but always faces it so he can see an approaching threat. That is why, even when he sleeps, he does not rest totally—part of him is always listening for sounds of danger.

He squats near the fire again. His heart is pounding in his chest. He is afraid; he is always afraid. But as he looks at his woman and his children, he knows he must never show them his fear. Without his courage, they would lose all hope. Without him, they are as good as dead. No, he must be strong. He must remember who he is. He is a man. He is a hunter.

The Displaced Warrior

The life of a man in modern society seems to bear no resemblance to the life lived by this primitive ancestor. And yet, up until not very long ago, man was still hunting and killing the food for his family; he had to be ready to defend them physically, whether against Indians or against the British.

Twentieth-century man doesn't need to hunt or fight. The skills for which he has been trained and bred for centuries are no longer necessary. There are no battles; there is no enemy; there is no challenge. He is the "displaced warrior."

Is it any wonder, then, that women voice the following complaints about the men in their lives?

> "He always seems so defensive—no matter what I say, he seems ready for a fight."

> "He has such a hard time opening up and showing me his feelings—it's as if he always has to look so strong."

> "I wish my husband would reach out to other men for friendship, but he can't seem to get close to men."

> "Bob takes his work so seriously that it drives me crazy. I try to get him to lighten up about it, but he acts like it's a matter of life and death whether he gets a report done today or tomorrow."

> "My boyfriend gets so angry when he feels he's being criticized or mistreated or challenged by someone— he interprets any kind of disagreement as an attack, and he attacks back with sarcasm and by acting like a bully."

> "When my husband is upset about something, he just bottles it up inside. He becomes cold and distant, and it takes me days of nagging before he'll admit what's bothering him."

I'm sure you can see the remnants of the hunter-warrior mentality in the attitudes and behavior of these twentieth-century men. They are still being affected by forces within themselves that they may be totally unaware of. One theory is that human beings have a "genetic memory," some kind of consciousness passed down through the centuries that links an accountant living a quiet life in the suburbs with every relative he's ever had, all the way back to his primitive relatives of thousands of years ago.

▼

It's as if men "remember" those primitive impulses to defend, to never show weakness, to always stay in control, and unconsciously act these out in their everyday lives

▲

Why Men Choose Certain Seats in Restaurants

Several years ago I had an experience that absolutely convinced me that genetic memory must exist. At the time I was in a relationship with a man who was a teacher and a writer. Every time we'd go out for dinner, I'd notice something strange. We'd enter the restaurant, the waiter would show us to our table, and I would sit down in whatever chair the waiter held out for me. If my chair had its back to most of the restaurant, my partner would take the other chair. But if my chair was the one that offered a better view of the entire restaurant, my partner would look very uncomfortable and ask if we could switch seats. The first few times this occurred I didn't mind, and changed seats with him. But one night I was in kind of a stubborn mood, and when he asked if he could sit in the chair against the wall that looked out over the whole restaurant, I said, "No, I want this chair. You always get the nice views, and can watch everybody. This time I want to sit here."

My partner reluctantly agreed, and sat down in the chair opposite me with his back to the restaurant. We ordered our meal and I began talking about my day, and other light topics of conversation, when I noticed how uncomfortable he looked. He was literally squirming in his seat. "What's wrong?" I asked.

"I just don't like sitting here, I can't relax," he replied.

"I don understand—what's so terrible about sitting in that chair?"

"I can't see anything," he explained, "and I feel funny having my back to the room like this—it makes me nervous."

For the next half hour we analyzed the funny feeling my partner had about sitting with his back toward the room, and what we discovered surprised us both. Although this man had never thought about it before, he always made a point of sitting so he could see whatever room he was in, whether in a restaurant or at a party. Although his rational mind knew there was no actual threat of danger in these situations, he still did not feel safe with his back turned—it went against something very deep inside him to even think about sitting that way. It was as if he could hear a voice in his head warning, *Watch out! Stay alert!*

Now, this guy was not what you might consider a typically "macho" man—he was a gentle, scholarly person. He insisted that he'd never been trained to "sit defensively" by his father or by the army, and that until I'd pointed it out he'd never even been aware of what he was doing. We couldn't come up with any other explanation than the genetic memory theory—he knew he shouldn't turn his back to the "opening of the cave."

Since that time I've made a point of asking men about their seating choices in restaurants, and the majority of them agree that they do feel more comfortable sitting so they can have a clear view of the room, and do not like sitting with their backs to it. You might want to do your own research on this for fun. (Of course, if you ever want to make a man uncomfortable on purpose, insist that he take the seat with its back to the room, and watch him squirm!)

Why Men Have Always Dominated Women

Until the introduction of birth control, women's and men's roles were determined by the simple fact that women could get pregnant and bear children, and men could not. Let's look in on Jack and Jill Flintstone as they hunt and work together. If Jill doesn't want to be totally dominated by Jack, she'd better not have sex with him—because once she has sex, she'll get pregnant, and her equal status will disappear. Soon she will become heavy and be unable to run. Then she will have a baby and will have to nurse it and care for it, preventing her from going out and gathering food with Jack. By the time she has three or four children, she will become dependent on Jack for everything, since all of her time will be taken up with child care.

Meanwhile, Jack and all of his male friends have the ultimate power over the women for one reason—they find, kill, and distribute the meat. And the hunter who kills the most meat becomes the chief. If you're not nice to these guys, and you don't follow their rules, they can decide not to give you any meat, and you die. It's that simple. Perhaps this is why some men still become enraged at the thought of their wives going out to work; their ultimate form of control is threatened when she can bring home her own "bacon." Of course, centuries after men stopped hunting for their food, women were still bound to their homes because of their maternal and nursing capacities. The men had the economic power in the relationship—therefore, they were in control.

The Psychological Explanation for Why Men Dominate Women

Have you ever suspected that a man who was treating you badly and putting you down was secretly jealous of you, even threatened by you? Many theories suggest that men have been driven to dominate women because of a deep envy and awe of women's creative power. Women's bodies go through mysterious changes that men cannot understand; women seem to be endowed with certain intuitive and creative abilities men do not have; and most of all, women can conceive and give birth, certainly the most magical feat there is—all of these factors may contribute to the male need to dominate women.

More recent is the theory that male dominance grows out of a man's need to avoid identifying with the feminine and reflects every man's drive to break away from his mother. Because the mother is the primary model and relationship for a little boy, he will identify with her, with the feminine, unless he does something to separate himself from her. We've all seen this behavior in boys approaching puberty—they don't want to be kissed or touched by their mothers; they even insist they hate their mothers in an attempt to define themselves as different, as men. Nancy Chodorow, author of *The Reproduction of Mothering*, explains:

> Internally, the boy tries to reject his mother and deny his attachment to her and the strong dependency on her that he still feels . . . He does this by repressing whatever he takes to be feminine inside himself, and importantly, by denigrating whatever he considers to be feminine in the outside world.

▼

The rebellious little boy in men, still seeking to prove he is not his mother, continues to attempt to dominate women and see them as inferior as a way of saying, "See, since I have control over you, I am better than you. I am *not* you!"

▲

Later in this book, I'll explain how the little boy's desire for autonomy from Mommy still affects the behavior of the grown-up men we love.

How Men Are Trained to Be Unfit for Love

"It's a boy!" the doctor announces, and from that moment on, this tiny male person is treated differently from the baby girl in the next delivery room. Consider these facts, compiled from a variety of research studies.

▼ Parents of newborn male babies tend to describe their sons as *firmer, larger, more alert, stronger, and hardier.*

Parents of newborn female babies describe their daughters as *adorable, softer, smaller, prettier, and more delicate.* The parents actually believe their child exhibits these characteristics, even though according to the hospital reports, there is usually little or no difference between the two groups of infants.

▼ Parents tend to place more demands on little boys than on little girls, expecting them to be more responsible and take more risks.

▼ Parents push boys rather than girls to be independent. They offer less comfort to sons than to daughters when the child is frightened or injured, and they give boys greater freedom at an earlier age than they do girls.

▼ Parents encourage boys to control their emotions, and girls to express theirs. Boys are taught that it isn't manly to feel strong emotions, not only those emotions considered "weak" such as fear or sadness, but even passion, need, and intense love. In his book *Male Sexuality,* Dr. Bernie Zilbergeld describes how boys are trained to view showing their feelings:

> (They) learn early that only a narrow range of emotion is permitted . . . aggressiveness, competitiveness, anger, . . . and the feelings associated with being in control. As we grow older, sexual feelings are added to the list. Weakness, confusion, fear, vulnerability, tenderness, compassion and sensuality are allowed only to girls and women. A boy who exhibits any such traits is likely to be made fun of and called a sissy or a girl (and what could be more devastating?).

These days many new parents attempt to avoid stereotyping their children based on gender. But most of the adult men you and I are having relationships with are victims of this early-childhood conditioning.

How TV Teaches Us Sex Roles

As young children, most of us learned how to view ourselves as males and females not only from our parents but from the thousands of hours we spent watching television. There have been some fascinating studies of how men and women are portrayed on TV, and the results are disturbing:

▼ Male characters are generally shown in ambitious, adventuresome, strong, and dominant roles, while females are cast in dependent, submissive, and weak roles.

▼ Males are engaged in exciting activities for which they receive great rewards, while females are involved in activities that support or are less important than the men's, and for which they receive little reward.

▼ Television commercials present women as worried, tense, and concerned about problems such as toilet bowl odor, migraine headaches, and ring around the collar, while men are shown as authoritative, knowledgeable, and macho.

▼ The TV Western, a favorite with young boys in the 1950s and 60s, portrayed the all-American hero, the cowboy, as a loner, doing what needed to be done, riding off into the sunset alone, with no commitments, no ties—free.

Picture the man in your life during the years when he was a little boy, sprawled in front of the TV set watching program after program, and commercials in between, all depicting men as strong, cool, unemotional, always in control, afraid of nothing. Whether his hero was the Lone Ranger, Zorro, Batman, Maverick, the boys of *Bonanza*, Peter Gunn, or any larger-than-life cowboy, detective or tough guy, your man knew how he wanted to be when he grew up. By the way, these programs never showed Zorro's wife, or the Long Ranger's girlfriend. No, for these TV role models, intimacy meant having a horse, or maybe a male sidekick, but never a woman.

In case the man in your life grew up with radio rather than TV, he isn't off the hook—radio dramas contained the same kinds of stereotypes as TV programs, which grew out of the radio days.

The Challenge of Changing Times

By now you're beginning to understand a lot more about why men are the way they are—why "to be a man" means to hide one's emotions, to fight off the competition, to struggle against the harsh world and survive, to cling to one's independence, to stay in control. Men are pulled by habits passed down from generation to generation, and are conditioned by their parents and society, which teach them values that close them off to intimacy.

▼

By deciding to be the "real man" society has taught him he must be, a man chooses to embody the very qualities that make it impossible for him to open up and experience true intimacy with the woman he loves

▲

This chart helps illustrate the tremendous emotional challenge men are facing today:

The Way Men Have Been Taught to Be	The Way We Ask Men to Be
Defensive and Suspicious	Trusting and Open
Hide Their Emotions	Show Their Emotions
Appear Strong and Unconquerable	Express Their Vulnerability
Competitive	Cooperative
Master the Outer World	Master the Inner World
Independent/the Loner	Feel Their Need for Us
Stays in Control	Let Go of Control

So here we are, women of the 1990s, telling the men in our lives that the characteristics they've worked so hard to cultivate are the very ones that drive us crazy and turn us off; and that the characteristics we really want to see them develop are the ones they have been taught to see as "weak" and "unmanly" and have fought so hard to avoid. When you think about it this way, it's a lot easier to understand why men seem to resist changing, why they feel that we're pressuring them unfairly, why they appear to be so bad at simple relationship skills that are so simple for us.

▼

We expect men to be competent in skills for which they have absolutely no training—the very skills, it so happens, that women are best at—the ability to express emotion, to be intimate, to nurture, and to love

▲

Over the past ten years I've worked with thousands of men, and I can assure you that men do want to open up, to learn to feel deeply and express those feelings to the women they love. But the process is a difficult, even frightening one for them, and I hope that, after reading this chapter, you can understand why. The men in your life need all of the compassion, patience, and support you can find in your heart, to help them open theirs.

The Chinese curse at the beginning of this chapter states: "May you live in changing times," and these times are certainly changing. The old ways of living and loving don't work anymore, and we still haven't figured out the new ways. In the meantime we're still trying to have relationships, and we're experiencing a lot of disappointment and confusion in the process. But the challenge of change lies in the incredible opportunity it offers us for new levels of wisdom and new heights of personal growth. This book is dedicated to helping you turn your challenges with men into exciting new adventures in loving.

2 | The Six Biggest Mistakes Women Make with Men

Do you ever suspect that everything you've been taught about how to behave with men is wrong?

▼

Do you ever do something you are sure will please a man, and feel shocked when he reacts to it so negatively?

▼

Do you ever feel that you must have received a bad set of "instructions" for how to successfully relate to men, because nothing you try seems to work the way it's supposed to?

If you answered yes to any of these questions, you're not alone. I've worked with thousands of women in my seminars and support groups, and most of them knew that there was something very wrong in the way they related to men but weren't sure what was wrong or how to change it. Part of improving your relationship with a man, whether it's your husband, your boss, your boyfriend, your father, or your coworker, is not just understanding his behavior but taking an honest look at your own behavior as well.

How Healthy Are Your Relationships with Men?

Here's a quiz designed to reveal the strengths and weaknesses in your relationships with the men in your life. For each question, select one of the following responses:

A. Almost always
B. Frequently
C. Occasionally
D. Rarely
E. Almost never

Answer each question as honestly as you can, choosing the response that applies to you most of the time. That means, don't answer based on how you know you *should* behave, but on how you *usually* behave.

1. When I'm around a man I really like or am attracted to, I lose part of myself by censoring my communications, seeking approval, sacrificing my needs, or becoming much more self-conscious.

2. I find myself feeling responsible for the men in my life, and making sure they get done what they need to.

3. I allow men to get away with treating me in ways I'd never tolerate being treated by a woman.

4. I use my sexuality to get my way with men by flirting, teasing, using body language, etc.

5. I allow my fear of how a man might react to prevent me from doing what I want to do or saying what I really feel around him.

6. I feel resentful toward men for things they've done to me in the past, or for how they treat me now.

7. I act helpless, overwhelmed, or confused around men to get love or attention or to avoid dealing with their anger toward me.

8. I feel I receive all the respect and appreciation I deserve from the men in my life.

9. I always ask for what I want and need from the men I care about.

10. When I'm around powerful men (boss, Dad, authority figures), I feel relaxed and confident in myself. I don't alter my behavior so that I appear either unusually pushy and aggressive or unusually timid.

Now, add up your total score. For questions 1 through 7, give yourself the following points:

A: 2 points
B: 4 points
C: 6 points
D: 8 points
E: 10 points

For questions 8 through 10, give yourself the following points:

A: 10 points
B: 8 points
C: 6 points
D: 4 points
E: 2 points

80–100 points: CONGRATULATIONS! Your hard work on yourself and your relationships has paid off, and you've learned how to be a powerful yet loving woman with the men in your life. You maintain a strong sense of yourself even when you're around men who are important to you, and you know that good communication is essential for creating healthy and lasting relationships. To avoid future problems, work on those areas in which you had a lower score.

60–79 points: YOUR RELATIONSHIPS WITH MEN AREN'T BAD, BUT THEY COULD BE A LOT BETTER. Most women fall into this category. There are some warning signs you need to pay attention to, so that in time bigger problems don't erupt. Work on expressing yourself and your needs more completely, and avoid the six mistakes women make with men, discussed later in this chapter. *You deserve much more love than you've been asking for.*

40–59 points: YOUR RELATIONSHIPS WITH MEN ARE IN SERIOUS TROUBLE. You have some bad emotional habits that are keeping you from receiving the love and appreciation you deserve. You'll never get the respect you want if you continue to give up your power around men, behave like a doormat and pretend everything is fine. It's time to make a change. The first step is to be honest with yourself about how dissatisfied you really are. Practice everything you learn from this book, ask your friends for support, and make a commitment to start living as the powerful woman you are meant to be.

39 points or below: EMERGENCY! YOUR RELATIONSHIPS WITH MEN ARE UNHEALTHY. You've been in pain and felt unloved for so long that you've probably forgotten what it feels like to be yourself around a man you really care about. You may not even know what a healthy relationship with a man is. It's time to take immediate action, and you can't do it alone. Reach out to other women for help; find a loving and experienced therapist; join some support groups; use this book as much as possible, and do whatever you can to begin to love yourself again. Fight off that numbness, negativity, and resentment. Stop playing the victim! Only you can make the change. You deserve much more than this.

I suggest you take this quiz over again from time to time to measure your progress in becoming a more powerful woman. First put the principles in this book into practice, and then come back to the quiz several weeks later. You should notice some real improvement reflected in a higher score, and you'll be well on your way to creating the loving relationships with men that you deserve.

Do You Bring Out the Worst In the Men You Love?

Whether you're aware of it or not, you may be bringing out the worst in the men you love by how you behave around them.

I am *not* saying that the problems in relationships are all the women's fault, or that how we behave is "wrong" or "bad," or that men don't need to change and we do. I *am* saying that how women act around men is 50 percent of the problem.

▼

Many of the behaviors we've adopted to try to be "loving women" are the very behaviors that are destructive to our relationships with men

▲

Of course, we don't make these mistakes on purpose. Most of us were taught these behavior patterns by our mothers, and their mothers before them, but when we act out these old roles and habits, they end up making us feel bad about ourselves as women, and actually encourage men to treat us badly.

THE 6 BIGGEST MISTAKES WOMEN MAKE WITH MEN

1   WOMEN ACT LIKE MOTHERS AND TREAT MEN LIKE CHILDREN

2   WOMEN SACRIFICE WHO THEY ARE AND PUT THEMSELVES SECOND IN IMPORTANCE TO THE MAN THEY LOVE

3   WOMEN FALL IN LOVE WITH A MAN'S POTENTIAL

4   WOMEN COVER UP THEIR EXCELLENCE AND COMPETENCE

5   WOMEN GIVE UP THEIR POWER

6   WOMEN ACT LIKE LITTLE GIRLS TO GET WHAT THEY WANT FROM MEN

MISTAKE 1

Women Act Like Mothers and Treat Men Like Children

Have you ever said any of the following things to a man?

"Honey, did you remember your wallet?"

"Don't forget to pick up the dry cleaning on the way home."

"Did you remember to pay that overdue electric bill?"

"Do you realize the gas tank is almost on empty?"

"You didn't remember to make reservations? Never mind, I'll call for you."

"How many times do I have to remind you not to leave
those wet towels on the floor?"
"Don't you think you're going to be cold with that light
jacket on?"

If you're like me, you're cringing with guilt after reading
this list. Mistake #1 is one of the most common and
destructive habits we have with men. We treat men like
children; we assume they can't take care of themselves; we
act as if they are incompetent, and that they need us to run
their lives for them.

Now, I know what you're thinking—that in many cases,
these assumptions are true! And you may be right. But that's
not the point. What's important is this:

▼

**WHEN YOU TREAT A MAN LIKE A LITTLE BOY, HE'S
GOING TO ACT LIKE A LITTLE BOY. WHEN YOU EXPECT
A MAN TO BE INCOMPETENT, HE REMAINS INCOMPE-
TENT**

▲

WAYS WOMEN ACT LIKE MOTHERS AND TREAT MEN
LIKE CHILDREN

**1. Acting overly helpful by doing things for men that
they should be doing for themselves.** We look for his
keys; pick up after him; go in the other room to get him
something he can easily find himself; straighten his tie; comb
his hair; choose his clothes for him in the morning and lay
them out on the bed.

**2. Playing verbal guessing games with men, trying to
pull information out of them.** We say, "Okay, you're
hungry . . . are you in the mood for cereal? No? What about
some pretzels? Not pretzels? Okay, then what about some

nice soup? Not appealing. Hmm, let me think . . . I know . . . what if I make you a grilled cheese sandwich? Wouldn't you like that?"

3. Assuming men will be absentminded or forgetful, and reminding them of information they should remember by themselves

"Don't forget to call me when you get there."

"Don't forget to pick up Susie at her dance class."

"Don't forget that it's trash night and the cans need to go out."

"Don't forget your doctor's appointment after work."

4. Scolding them as if they were children

"Where do you think you're going without a jacket? Don't you know how cold it is outside?"

"How many times do I have to tell you to turn the lights off before coming to bed. Our electric bill is outrageously high."

"You ate a whole pizza and had three beers at Herb's house while you watched the game? No wonder you have a stomach ache."

5. Taking charge of activities that you assume they can't do right

"If I let Fred make our dinner reservations, he somehow gets the time wrong, and forgets to request a good table, so I just do it myself."

"The last time I sent Steven clothes shopping with the kids, it was a disaster—they came home with stuff they could never wear to school. Now I just take them myself. I couldn't stand to go through that again."

"I asked Jason to find us a nice hotel in Chicago months ago, and wouldn't you know that it 'slipped his mind.'

Now our trip is three weeks away, and I'm the one who ends up making the phone calls anyway. I should have just done it myself in the first place."

6. Correcting and directing them

"No, honey, the couple we met on vacation was from Virginia, not West Virginia."

"The way you just used that word in a sentence was incorrect, dear."

"I think if you take Route 41 to the expressway, we'll avoid the traffic on Grant Avenue. In fact, I'd get in the left lane now if I were you."

"Why don't you just call your mother up, and first tell her that the kids aren't feeling well, and then mention how busy you are this week at the office. After she starts to feel concerned, then let her know that we've decided not to come to visit next Sunday. But whatever you do, don't tell her we saw my mother last weekend."

WHY WOMEN MOTHER MEN

I know you hate to think you might be taking a mothering role with the man you love, but believe me, you're not alone. Why do we act like mommies and treat our men like children?

▼ **Women are trained to be mothering and are rewarded for it.** When you were growing up, your primary role model was your mother. Watching her take care of you and your brothers or sisters, you learned how to be nurturing, giving, selfless, and attentive to the needs of others. If your mother also played a mommy role with your father, this conditioning was even more powerfully reinforced. Look at it this way: If you almost always saw Mom treat Dad in a mothering way, rather than in a romantic way, you assumed as a child that this is how women are supposed to behave with men. When you grew up and found yourself in a relationship with a man, you unconsciously started mothering him, since that was how you'd been taught women act with men.

Julie had been married to Fred for three years when she came to me complaining about her relationship. "I don't feel like Fred's wife," she said bitterly, "I feel like his mother! He seems to act like such a baby around me, expecting me to pick up after him, think for him, and be the one who ends up in charge. He's getting lazier and lazier, and I'm getting more and more angry!"

Julie wasn't even aware of how natural it was for her to mother Fred. She'd been blaming him for being immature for so long, that she'd never taken a look at her part in creating the problem. As we talked about her parents, we could both see the roots of Julie's mommy game. "I can't ever remember my mother and father being intimate or romantic with each other," Julie recalled sadly. "My dad traveled a lot for his business, and my most vivid and common memories of my mother are of her packing for him before his trips, unpacking for him after his trips, making sure he remembered to keep his appointments when he was in town, and constantly fussing over his clothes. I guess by the time we were in our early teens, Dad was kind of like one of the kids. Mom would scold us and scold him; she'd shove lunches at us and shove his lunch at him. I never realized that, on some level, I must have concluded that loving a man meant treating him like Mom treated Dad."

Until recently, being a mother was one of the only acceptable "professions" for women with nurse and teacher close behind. We grew up seeing our mothers rewarded for their nurturing behavior, and getting rewarded for that same behavior in ourselves: "Good Sally, you're taking care of your little brother so nicely." "Be a sweetheart, Jane, and bring Daddy his slippers—that's my girl."

▼
WE OFTEN RETURN TO OUR MOTHERING BEHAVIOR WHEN WE WANT TO BE LOVED BY A MAN
▲

Darlene, married for fifteen years, described it this way: "Whenever I feel like I'm not getting enough attention from Charlie, I definitely fall back into the mothering mode—I start baking his favorite dishes, or organizing his drawers for him, or trying to be as helpful as I can. What I really want is more affection, more intimacy, for him to act like more of a lover and not just a husband. Of course, this is the opposite of what I get—the grateful 'son' thanking me for being so considerate."

▼ **We mother men in order to become indispensable to them.** When you work hard to fulfill all of a man's needs, he becomes increasingly dependent on you. We've all seen the television commercials that show the man trying to make dinner for the kids on his wife's night out. He's depicted as an incompetent idiot who is helpless around the house without his wife. The more you take care of a man, the more he relies on you and the more indispensable you become. As women, we often deal with our fear of loss and abandonment by attempting to make men so dependent on us that they would never consider leaving us. It's as if our unconscious mind thinks, *If he needs me enough, he'll never leave me.*

▼ **Men are accustomed to being mothered and love the feeling of being taken care of.**
Recently, I was giving a seminar to a group of women and I asked a rhetorical question of the audience, "Why do women mother men?" Someone way in the back shouted, "Because men love it!" Everyone laughed because we all knew that there was a lot of truth in what she had said. Will men complain when you mother them? Sometimes—but not most of the time.

▼
MEN WILL FEEL LOVED WHEN YOU MOTHER THEM
▲

Men grow up with their mommies taking care of them, and they find it very easy as adults to allow the women in their lives to continue playing that maternal role. This is especially true of your man if he saw his mother treat his own father like a child. He might even associate the idea of "wife" with mother, caretaker, and nurturer, rather than lover, best friend, or partner. And if the man in your life didn't get all of the love and attention he needed from his own mother when he was a little boy, he'll gladly allow you to "finish the job."

How Mothering the Man in Your Life Can Destroy Your Relationship

Acting out a mothering role with men might appear to have its rewards at first, but in reality, it will have some very devastating effects on your relationship.

1. Your man will end up resenting you and rebelling against you. In Chapter 1 we talked about the psychological need every little boy has to assert his independence from Mommy in order to define himself as a male and not a female. When you take on a mothering role with your man, it's inevitable that your man will begin to resent you, and eventually he will rebel against you. He may not complain about your behavior; he may insist that he doesn't want you to stop; but he will end up rebelling, because all boys have to break away from Mommy someday.

Karen, 52, came to me after she discovered her husband was having an affair with a 24-year-old secretary from his office. Karen couldn't understand why her husband, Leonard, had strayed from the marriage. "He always seemed so content," she explained as she sat in my office. "I know I spoiled him—he used to say that he hadn't even gotten this kind of treatment from his own mother—but he insisted that he loved being pampered and coddled. Now he tells me he felt stifled, trapped in the relationship, and that he wants his freedom. He never complained for twenty-seven years. I just don't understand what happened."

When I talked with Leonard, my suspicions were confirmed—he felt he was trading in a mother for a lover by leaving his wife and choosing a younger woman. Even the words he used to describe his relationship with Karen—"trapped, stifled, longing for his freedom"—sound like those of a teenage boy who can't wait to leave home and be on his own. Karen thought she was being a good wife by mothering Leonard, but in the end it drove him away.

2. Your man will end up feeling incompetent. When you continually treat a man as if he is incompetent, he begins to feel incompetent. The more incompetent he feels, the lower his self-esteem, and the more he will actually behave incompetently. This creates a vicious circle:

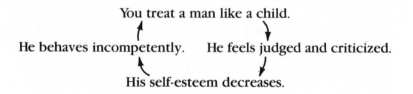

WHEN A MAN DOES NOT FEEL GOOD ABOUT HIMSELF, HE WILL BECOME LESS LOVING TO YOU

A man's self-worth comes from his sense of competence. And when a man feels he is not doing a good job in any area of his life, it becomes very difficult for him to be loving toward himself or you. Emphasizing a man's incompetence by treating him like a child is guaranteed to inhibit his ability to love you.

The other side of this is that the more incompetent your man appears to you, the more turned off to him you will become. Women are turned on by competence. So the more inept he seems, the less attractive he'll be.

3. You will kill the passion in the relationship.

▼
THE QUICKEST WAY TO KILL THE PASSION IN YOUR RELATIONSHIP IS TO MOTHER THE MAN YOU LOVE
▲

The more you act like a man's mother, the more he will treat you like his mother. But no man wants to sleep with his mother. The sexual taboo against feeling attracted to a female with mothering energy is so deeply rooted in most men that it will be impossible for your partner to continue to see you in an erotic, romantic way when you are constantly picking lint off of his clothes, reminding him to do his chores, and otherwise treating him like your son.

Of course, treating your man like a child will turn you off as well. How romantic can you feel at the end of the day when you see your man and think to yourself, *He couldn't find his socks; he lost his keys again; I had to call the plumber because he forgot*? How excited can you get about someone who you've just finished treating like a three-year-old?

I believe that Mistake #1 is one of the primary causes for the lack of a satisfying sex life in many marriages. Being together for twenty years, having financial pressures, bringing up a family—these all contribute to the tension that can inhibit passion. But none of them are as destructive as the transformation of the husband and wife into a mother and her son.

The Solution: How to Stop Mothering Men

Here are some suggestions for transforming yourself from a mother into a lover with your man.

1. Stop doing things for your man that he should be doing for himself. Treating men like children is like an addiction, and like any addiction the only way to stop is to *Stop.* This means that when your husband asks you where his keys are, say "I don't know," and let him look for them himself. When he is ready to get dressed for a certain occasion, don't suggest what clothes he should wear. When he leaves a pile of clothes lying on the floor, don't pick them up for him.

If your man is used to your doing things for him, he is going to have to adjust to your new role. At first, it might be difficult. You may have to put up with his frustration as he learns to do things for himself that he hasn't in years. And don't be surprised if your life temporarily becomes a little more chaotic. You may be late for a party because he can't find his keys. He may leave the house with his tie crooked. But when these things happen often enough, he'll learn. He'll remember how frustrated he was looking for his keys and will learn to put them in the same place every night. He'll recall how many times he's told his tie is crooked and will learn to check it in the mirror himself. In other words, he'll grow up and learn to take care of himself.

Of course, this doesn't mean that the next time your husband asks you if you've seen his keys you should respond, "Find them yourself! I'm not your mother!" And I don't believe you should stop being loving, nurturing, and supportive to your partner. It simply means being more of a wife or mate, and less of a mommy.

2. Treat your man like a competent, reliable person. Don't remind him of information he should remember. Don't be his brain and his calendar for him. Act as if he is a competent adult who can be counted on. Remember, your man might have gotten lazy since you've been doing a lot of the scheduling for him; he may unconsciously rely on you to make sure he doesn't forget important appointments or responsibilities. So when you stop mothering him, he may find himself missing meetings, forgetting to pay bills, or neglecting to take out the cans on trash night. If this happens, do not scold him or criticize him, just sympathize with his frustration, and go about your own business.

Let's say your partner has a dentist appointment on a Thursday. Say good-bye to him Thursday morning as usual. On Thursday evening, he comes home and announces "I'm so mad at myself. Dr. Hopkins's office called me at work and told me I had an appointment today. I totally forgot about it." You respond by saying, "That's too bad, honey. I'm sure you can reschedule." *After enough missed appointments and forgotten events, your partner will learn to keep better track of his own schedule.*

3. Don't speak to your partner in "mommy-talk." Promise yourself that you'll stop talking to your man as if he is a five-year-old. That means: *No Scolding!* It's perfectly all right for you to let your partner know when you are upset or angry. But talk to him as one adult to another, not as an exasperated mother to her bad little boy.

What about "baby talk" in a relationship? I think some baby talk is natural, an intimate way we share our vulnerable selves with each other. If you and your partner speak in baby talk a lot of the time, however, especially in bed or during sex, then you've got a problem. It's time to have a grown-up relationship.

4. Decide what responsibilities you want him to handle in the relationship, and don't take over even when he makes a mistake. I know how difficult it's going to be for many of you to do this. It means letting go of control and trusting things to work out all right in the end, even if they don't happen as you would have liked them to. For instance, your husband says he will make reservations for dinner one evening, but he calls the restaurant too late in the day, and all the tables are booked. When he telephones you at six o'clock to say he couldn't get reservations, you say, "That's too bad. I'll be ready at eight o'clock as planned. I'm sure you can find some place for us to go. See you then." He'll feel stupid for procrastinating, grateful that you didn't berate him, and will remember this feeling the next time he plans to take you out for dinner.

Warning: You will be tempted to intervene when you see the situation falling apart. Your vacation is coming up, and you know your husband hasn't made plane reservations yet. Or your boyfriend decides to make some lasagna, and you know he is putting in too much sauce.

▼
DON'T GIVE IN TO THE TEMPTATION TO RESCUE HIM
▲

Let him make his own mistakes, and live with the consequences. That's the only way he will learn to do things differently next time.

How I Stopped a Man from "Driving" Me Crazy

Having spent fifteen years of my adult life mothering men, I consider myself, unfortunately, an expert on the subject, and want to share a story about breaking the mommy habit. I was in a relationship with a man who was chronically forgetful. He'd forget his appointments; he'd forget to return phone calls; he'd forget to mail in bills; he'd even forget where he was going when we were driving somewhere, and would miss the correct exit on the freeway. For two years, I took on the responsibility of being his brain, reminding him of what to do and where to go in his life. Whenever we'd drive somewhere, I'd never relax—I'd be on the lookout for each exit and appropriate turn, to make sure we got to our destination on time.

Finally, I got fed up with mothering him and decided that the only way he was going to learn to pay attention on the road was if I stopped doing it for him. One weekend we took a trip to a spa in southern California. We'd been there before and, of course, I knew the exact directions. We'd been driving for about an hour when we reached the signs that indicated that our turn-off was a few miles ahead. I glanced at my partner to see if he'd noticed, and felt my stomach tightening up. *No!* I warned myself. *You promised you weren't going to say anything.* The closer we got to the exit, the more of a nervous wreck I became. And then we were at the exit, and my partner kept on driving. He'd missed it! I clenched my teeth tightly together to keep myself from screaming.

Time seemed to stand still as we drove ten miles, twenty miles, thirty miles past where we should have turned off. It was beginning to get dark. Suddenly he turned to me and said, "Does this area look familiar to you?"

"No," I replied softly.

"I didn't think it did," he said. "Maybe I missed the turn-off." He stopped at a gas station and found out that, sure enough, he had just driven forty miles out of his way, making us late for our arrival at the spa. It took all my self-control not to say anything. As my partner turned the car around and headed back in the other direction, he looked at me sheepishly and said, "You knew I'd missed the exit, didn't you?" I smiled at him; he smiled back. We both knew that he'd learned more of a lesson from driving forty miles in the middle of nowhere than he would have if I'd intervened and pointed out his mistake.

5. Make a list: "The Ways I Play Mommy . . ." Sit down and write out all of the ways you play Mommy in your relationships. Watch yourself over a few weeks, and add to the list whenever you catch yourself. If you're really brave, ask your partner to suggest items that should go on the list! You may be surprised at how long your list turns out to be. *The first step in changing your behavior is becoming aware of it.*

6. Talk with the man in your life about the mommy/ son games you play together, and work as a team to create a grown-up relationship. I suggest you give this book to the man in your life, so that he can understand you and himself better. Have some serious discussions about everything you've read in this chapter so far, and ask him for his input on the topic. Then make some agreements together, guidelines you each agree to follow that will help you create a grown-up relationship.

7. Be consistent. It's essential to be consistent in following your new rules and avoiding the old mistakes. Stick to your commitments, no matter what the consequences. For instance, you agree not to clean up after your husband in his bathroom, and that he is responsible for taking his own underwear and towels into the laundry room. After one week you notice that there is a huge pile of clothing in the middle of his bathroom floor, and that he has no clean towels left on his shelf and no underwear in his drawer. *Don't touch that dirty pile of clothes!* Wait until he complains that there are no clean towels, or that he has no underwear to put on, and remind him that all his towels and underwear are still on the floor where he left them. He may not be in the greatest mood, but he'll get the message. If you give in for your own sense of sanity and orderliness, he'll never take your new commitment seriously, and won't stick to his.

Remember, it's not easy to break the mothering habit, but when you do, you will feel like more of a woman, and your partner will look and feel like more of a man.

MISTAKE **2**

Women Sacrifice Who They Are and Put Themselves Second in Importance to the Man They love

You've just spent several hours preparing a special dinner for your partner, fillet of sole almondine. You're about to bring the two plates to the table when you realize that one of the portions of fish is larger than the other. Assuming you and your mate have equal appetites, will you give him the bigger portion, or keep it for yourself?

Most women to whom I pose this question sheepishly admit that they wouldn't even have to give this dilemma much thought—of course they'd give the bigger portion to the man, because they are so used to putting the man first and themselves second. In fact, many women I interviewed said they'd actually feel *guilty* taking the larger piece of fish; they used words like *selfish, stingy, unloving.*

Mistake #2 has to do with how we as women sacrifice who we are, and put ourselves second in importance to the men in our lives. How do we do this?

1. We give up our own interests, hobbies, and activities. Sara, 31, used to be very involved in studying and practicing meditation and yoga. She found it helped her relax, and kept her feeling healthy. Then she met Bill, 36, a computer consultant, who had a cynical and skeptical attitude toward "that Eastern stuff," as he called it. In order to avoid conflict, she stopped going to her yoga retreats one weekend a month, and found she was skipping more and more of her regular meditations, until she stopped entirely. When asked why she gave up these interests, she answered, "I guess I'm in a different phase of my life now. I've kind of outgrown those things."

A year and a half later, Sara and Bill broke up. Within two weeks, Sara finds herself beginning to meditate again. "I can't believe how much I missed this," she remarked.

Emily has always loved to dance. She took ballet and jazz when she was growing up, and enjoyed going dancing on the weekends with friends. Dancing makes her feel alive, graceful, and free. When Emily was 29 she met Andrew, 31. They began dating, fell in love, and got married two years later. I recently bumped into Emily at a department store, and after asking her how she and Andrew were doing, I mentioned dancing. Emily looked uncomfortable and replied, "Well, I don't do much dancing anymore." When I asked her why, she explained: "You see, Andrew has never really liked dancing. He's always felt like a klutz, and in the beginning I would drag him to clubs with me, but he'd just sit there all night and refuse to get up on the dance floor. It wasn't fun seeing him sulk, so we stopped going. He encouraged me to go dancing without him, not to sacrifice on his account. I went once or twice with some friends, but I felt guilty leaving him home alone. I guess I miss dancing, but it's no big deal, really."

These women are doing what many of us do—*giving up our own interests and hobbies because they are not important to the man in our life.* We don't even realize that we are making these sacrifices. We convince ourselves that we aren't really missing anything, that it doesn't matter. But it does. Often we become aware that we have made our own choices and activities second best only after the relationship has ended, and we find ourselves taking up those interests again. Then we remember how much we used to enjoy meditating, or dancing, or gardening, or cycling, or whatever it is that we gave up because the man in our life wasn't particularly interested in it.

2. We give up friends or family members our partner doesn't approve of. JoAnne, 26, was a beautician, who met her boyfriend, Lawrence, a 30-year-old antique dealer, at a swap meet. JoAnne was bubbly, clever, and vivacious, and even though she'd never gone to college, she had good "street smarts" and was doing well in business. Lawrence had graduated with honors from an East Coast Ivy League university, and considered himself an intellectual. The problems between them began the first time JoAnne took Lawrence to a friend's birthday party. JoAnne was having a wonderful time until she looked over and saw Lawrence sitting by himself. "What's wrong, honey?" she asked.

"I don't really feel comfortable here," Lawrence answered with a scowl. "I really have nothing in common with these friends of yours."

On the way home in the car, JoAnne and Lawrence argued about the party. "I hate you thinking my friends aren't good enough for you," JoAnne yelled. "So what if they didn't go to college—they're really good people."

"Look, if you want to spend time with them, that's your business," Lawrence replied. "Just don't expect me to participate."

JoAnne was furious at Lawrence for his superior attitude, but she secretly wondered if he was right, if her friends weren't good enough for her. She was afraid of what would happen if she continued to see them. Would Lawrence break up with her? Over the next few months she began to spend less and less time with her old friends, until she stopped seeing them entirely. She felt lonely—but after all, she had Lawrence.

Jackie's parents had never approved of Mike when Jackie dated him in college, and they were even more upset when the couple decided to move in together. Mike was a heavy drinker, and even though he claimed he could stop any time he wanted to, he never seemed to want to. Jackie loved Mike, and knew he loved her, but was afraid to really confront him about his drinking. Jackie had always been very close to her parents, since she was an only child, but all that began to change once she and Mike started living together. Each time Jackie would mention that she'd spoken to her mother or father, Mike would start complaining that Jackie was still depending too much on her parents, that she was acting like a little girl, and that she needed to break away from them and be her own person. Jackie loved her parents, but she didn't want to lose Mike, so she began to taper off her phone calls and visits with them, until she hardly had any contact with them at all. Mike told Jackie that he was proud of her for being so "strong." But Jackie drives by her parents' house every week, parks the car across the street, and cries.

If I asked you, "Would you reject a friend or family member if a man asked you to?" you'd probably answer with a resounding *"No Way!"* And yet many women do just that. They turn their backs on people who are important to them rather than risk the loss of a man's love.

Why do some men try to separate you from people who care about you?

▼

MEN WHO ARE INSECURE WITHIN THEMSELVES WILL TRY TO CUT YOU OFF FROM YOUR SUPPORT SYSTEMS

▲

There are men who need to feel they have total control over their partner, who are frightened of being controlled themselves. One of their tactics for exerting that power over you might be to cut you off from those people and groups who love and support you—your family, your friends, your church or spiritual group. This can have two results.

1. You become more dependent on the man for love, since you're getting less of it from other sources.

2. Your relationship becomes isolated from the scrutiny of the people who love you, thereby protecting your partner from possible criticism and negative feedback about his treatment of you.

3. We become "emotional chameleons," walking into the relationship like a blank slate, and becoming whatever the man wants us to be. One of the most common ways women put themselves second is by being willing to sacrifice who they are, and become whatever their man wants them to be. I call this being an "emotional chameleon," willing to change yourself, your looks, your behavior, and even your beliefs in order to fit your man's image of his ideal woman. *I'll be the woman of his dreams,* we decide, and we proceed to mold ourselves into someone else's picture of what is lovable.

Here's a true and sad story about how one woman sacrificed her entire personality for a man. Janice, a 32-year-old singer, walked into my office full of bitterness and rage. She'd just ended a three-year relationship with Tony, a telephone repairman. "Do you know what I did every weekend for three years?" she asked me. "I went to wrestling matches. Not to a movie, or the theater, but to goddamn wrestling matches. And when we were home, what do you think we watched on TV? Wrestling. I knew every wrestler, I knew who hated whom, I knew all the moves."

"I don't understand," I replied. "You still haven't told me what the problem was."

Janice looked at me with daggers in her eyes and growled, *"I hate wrestling!* In fact, I hate sports. But Tony loved it, and whatever Tony wanted, I did. I became a wrestling groupie just to please him. I even convinced myself that I liked it. I thought of it as a 'love sacrifice.' Now, whenever I think about it even for a second, I want to throw up. I am so pissed off at myself for being such an idiot."

Janice had walked into her relationship with Tony a blank slate, willing to alter her personality in exchange for love. Living in Los Angeles, I often meet women who are making this unfortunate mistake in extreme ways, to the point of altering their physical appearance with plastic surgery because the man they're involved with wants them to look different. I've counseled dozens of women who were "instructed" by their men to have their breasts enlarged or their backsides lifted, went ahead with the surgery, and are now dealing with their feelings of rage and humiliation.

4. We give up our own dreams, in order to help a man make his dreams come true. The wife who drops out of school to support her husband while he becomes a doctor, and realizes, fifteen years later, that she forgot about her own dreams of teaching retarded children. . . .

The woman who quits her job in a major corporation to help her boyfriend with the bookkeeping for his import business, only to realize when they break up three years later that she did it for him and not for herself, and that now she has nothing to show for it. . . .

I'm sure that if you haven't done this yourself, you know a woman who has. It's so sad that as women we are so willing to give up own dreams and adopt those of the man we love.

WHY WOMEN SACRIFICE THEMSELVES IN RELATIONSHIPS

Perhaps this question seems unnecessary to you. As a friend of mine put it, "Honey, sacrifice is my middle name!" There are several reasons women sacrifice themselves so readily with men.

▼ Men expect us to put ourselves second. They've been trained for thousands of years to think of women as second-class citizens, as less important. After all, we live in a world where, in many countries, women still have to walk behind their man on the street as a sign of subservience. Is it any wonder, then, that men expect us to be the one to sacrifice?

▼ **We've been trained as women to put ourselves second.** Many of us watched our mothers and grandmothers sacrifice their talents, interests, dreams and careers in order to be a support system for our fathers. We've been taught that putting ourselves first is "selfish."

▼ **We glamorize sacrifice as some kind of achievement, rather than going out and making our real dreams come true.** It's so much easier, and less personally challenging, to say: "Well, I would have gotten my degree and become an attorney, but I wanted to be there for Henry when he was in law school, so I decided to make the sacrifice."

The Results of Sacrificing for Love

When you sacrifice for love and put yourself second in a relationship, you believe inside that your man will end up loving you more. This may or may not happen. But what will happen is:

------------------------▼------------------------

WHEN YOU SACRIFICE WHO YOU ARE IN ORDER TO BE LOVED MORE BY SOMEONE ELSE, YOU END UP LOVING YOURSELF LESS

------------------------▲------------------------

Each time you give up an interest, a friend, or a dream in the hope of winning a man's love, you give away a piece of yourself. The more you sacrifice, the less of yourself remains, until one day you wake up and you feel empty. There is nothing of you left. You've cut it all away to become more acceptable, and in the process you've lost your essence, the soul of your womanhood.

This loss is almost always followed by anger or depression. You feel so much resentment toward yourself for what you have done, and an enormous loss of your self-respect and self-esteem. And you feel resentment towards the man you sacrificed for who, more times than not, didn't end up loving you the way you wanted to be loved anyway.

The Solution: How to Stop Sacrificing Yourself in Relationships

1. Make a list of all the ways you have sacrificed for love in every relationship you've ever been in. This is NOT a fun exercise to do, but I highly recommend it as a powerful technique for getting you motivated and disgusted enough so that you will stop putting yourself second once and for all.

2. Make a list of people, interests, activities, and beliefs that are important to you. This will help you remember who you are and what you care about. It will be a lot more difficult for you to convince yourself that you really do enjoy dirt-bike racing, or fishing, or stamp collecting, or whatever the next man you meet is into.

3. Make a commitment to your own dreams, so you can become full in yourself, rather than an empty "emotional chameleon," waiting to be filled up by a man. The more complete and whole you are as a woman, the less likely it is that you will walk into a relationship desperate for validation and therefore a likely candidate for sacrifice. In the final chapter of the book, I'll give you some suggestions for becoming the powerful woman you know you can be.

MISTAKE **3** _____

Women Fall in Love with a Man's Potential

Do you pride yourself on your ability to "bring out the best in a man"?

Have you ever told yourself that, with "a little time and work," the man you love will become just what you want him to be?

Have you ever felt that the reason your man hasn't become as successful as he wants to be is that he hasn't had anyone to "really love and support him"— that is, until you came along?

I don't know about you, but these questions look painfully familiar to me. Until recently, I made a profession out of Mistake #3—falling in love with a man's potential. I was an expert at finding men in need, and focusing much of my time and energy on "helping" them, "fixing" them. Sometimes my efforts were successful, and the man would become successful. Sometimes my efforts failed. But every time, the same thing occurred in my life: *I got to avoid my own career, my own dreams by attempting to rescue someone else.*

For as long as I can remember, I'd always chosen men who needed fixing in a particular area of their life. Some needed to be emotionally opened up. Some needed to heal the pain of a difficult childhood. Some needed to stop procrastinating, get organized, and use their talents to make money. Some needed to improve their speaking ability or writing skills, or learn how to dress correctly, or how to be an attentive lover. So, I would come to the rescue. I would offer them direction and advice to sort out their confusion. I would give them my love, my money, my energy, and my advice. My friends and family would express their disapproval and tell me I was wasting my time, but that didn't stop me. And even if the men didn't seem to be improving, or didn't appear to want my help, I wouldn't give up. After all, I'd made a commitment.

Looking back, I realize that each time, I wasn't really in a relationship—I was working on a project. And I wasn't involved with a man—I was dedicated to a cause.

▼

I WASN'T IN LOVE WITH THE MAN AS HE ACTUALLY WAS—I WAS IN LOVE WITH HIS POTENTIAL

▲

After many years of frustration, heartache, and disappointment, I woke up one day and realized that I was in my early thirties, and still hadn't accomplished my own career goals.

That's when I said to myself, "Barbara, if you'd put even half the amount of energy, creativity, and commitment into *your own goals and your own life* that you've put into helping men unfold their potential, there's no telling how successful and fulfilled you could become!" And that's what I did, and you're experiencing part of the result right now as you read this book.

How We Fall in Love with a Man's Potential

1. We go on "emotional rescue missions," finding men who aren't willing to help themselves, and attempt to "save" them.

Allison, a 32-year-old real-estate salesperson, came to me for career counseling. The more we talked, the more apparent it became that her problem wasn't with her real-estate job, but with her other full-time "job"—taking care of

Harry. Allison had been living with Harry, a 37-year-old actor, for three years. "I love Harry so much," she explained. "He had a really rough childhood, and a first marriage that was just awful, so when I met him, he was very insecure and abusive to himself. He's a good actor, he really is, but he's had a hard time finding work. He used to do a lot of cocaine and smoke cigarettes. I got him to stop, so that's been good. Now I'm working with him on setting well-defined goals and sticking to a schedule. I'm sure you probably think I'm crazy for being with him, but I just know that he could be really successful, I can feel it."

Allison believed in Harry more than he believed in himself. She loved the potential in him, not the man he was living as from day to day. In some part of Allison's mind, she'd decided that she would be successful when Harry got his life together. So no matter how well she did in her own career, she felt like a failure as long as Harry wasn't progressing according to her plan.

2. We find men who don't love us or treat us well, and hold out for the piece we aren't getting that we know is in there.

Erika, 45, was a perfect example of a woman making Mistake #3. She'd been married to Arnold for nineteen years, and had never been happy for all that time. "I not only fell in love with Arnold's potential," she admitted tearfully, "I married it! Arnold has never been a very loving, giving person. He's emotionally closed off and very critical. But inside of him, there is this sweet, frightened little boy who comes out once in a while and who just wants to be loved. When we were dating, I'd see glimpses of that part of him, and just melt. I remember the night he proposed to me, he broke down and cried for the first time since I'd known him. I realized that he had problems, but I figured, 'If I just love him enough, he will open up.' My parents disapproved of the marriage, but I told them they didn't know Arnold like I did.

"Well, nineteen years and three kids later, Arnold hasn't

changed a bit. I've spent most of our marriage feeling unloved and unappreciated, and I can't take it anymore. I still love him, and I still see that beautiful part inside of him, but I'm finally facing the fact that he just isn't going to change. I know I'm making the right decision in leaving him, but somehow I feel if only I'd loved him more or helped him more, maybe he would have opened up."

Erika spent her life longing for that piece of Arnold he was withholding, rather than telling herself the truth about what he was really willing to give her in the relationship. I know just how Erika felt, because I did exactly that in one of my own relationships. I spent several years with someone I loved very much, who not only wasn't living his own potential, but wasn't giving me that last piece of his heart, that last 10 percent of emotional surrender and commitment. And like Erika, I set myself up for failure by thinking:

------------------------------- ▼ -------------------------------

IF I LOVE HIM ENOUGH, HE WILL CHANGE

------------------------------- ▲ -------------------------------

The truth is, if a man loves *himself* enough, he will change!

Women who fall in love with a man's potential often don't feel good about themselves and think they need to perform in order to be loved by someone else. We choose men who are emotionally challenging and then set out to love them *in spite of who they are.* Then we get to say, "Look how loving, patient, tolerant, and compassionate I am. I must be lovable, right?"

I finally learned that:

------------------------------- ▼ -------------------------------

HAVING A HEALTHY RELATIONSHIP WITH A MAN MEANS LOVING HIM FOR WHO HE IS *NOW,* AND NOT LOVING HIM *IN SPITE OF* WHO HE IS TODAY, OR *IN HOPES OF* WHO HE WILL BE TOMORROW

------------------------------- ▲ -------------------------------

Why Women Fall in Love With a Man's Potential

▼ We get to avoid taking care of our own lives and facing our own destinies by deciding that we are responsible for helping someone else.

▼ We get to feel good about ourselves by demonstrating how helpful, loving, and patient we are.

▼ We get to feel like a failure and punish ourselves for not being perfect when our man doesn't turn out the way we thought he would.

▼ Women love to take things and make them better! We love doing makeovers on houses, people's hair, or whatever! It's an expression of that urge to create that is so natural to us. It's hard for a woman to resist improving on something.

How to Tell if You Are a "Rescue-holic"

Here are some warning signs to watch out for that may indicate you are making Mistake #3:

▼ Telling yourself that your man just needs a little more time to get himself and his life together, and doing this every few months.

▼ Telling yourself that no one has ever really loved your man enough, and that you will be the one to love him enough to change him.

▼ Feeling that everyone else misunderstands your man and that only you know the "real" person inside of him—"You don't know him like I do."

▼ Making excuses to your friends and family about why your man either isn't treating you well or isn't doing well himself.

▼ Feeling that you can't give up on this man and leave him, because it will just validate his feelings of worthlessness, and then he'll never change.

▼ Convincing yourself that, even though your man doesn't give you that piece of himself and his heart, what he does give you makes it worth staying in the relationship.

THE SOLUTION: HOW TO STOP FALLING IN LOVE WITH
A MAN'S POTENTIAL

As a recovering "rescue-holic," let me give you some suggestions for healing yourself of this painful pattern.

1. Focus your creative energies on your own life and career first, rather than on your man's. Make a list of your dreams and goals, and a concrete plan for attaining them. Stick to your own schedule, and beware of getting sidetracked. This means that if you plan to attend a networking meeting that can help you get more clients for your business, but your boyfriend needs help fixing up his apartment, go to your meeting! Know what you want in life before you even get involved in a new relationship, so that your agenda comes first.

2. Make a list: "The things I'm avoiding in my life by rescuing men." Often you won't be aware of how many of your own emotions or challenges *you* are avoiding by rescuing men. Making a list will help focus your attention on these hidden areas.

3. Find a man who wants to take responsibility for fixing himself, so that you don't have to do the work for him. There's nothing wrong with supporting the man you love in his personal growth and helping him make the changes he wants to make. When two people really love one another, both of them help bring out the hidden potential in the other. But it's important that you work as a team—that your man is as committed to working on himself as you are.

I suggest that, in the beginning of a relationship, you ask a man what his personal goals are, and how he plans to achieve them. You might find out that even though you want him to become more emotional or expressive, he has no interest in developing that way. Then you'd know he's not for you. If he does claim he wants to grow in the same ways you'd like to see him grow, give him some time, love, and support, and evaluate him in a few months. If you haven't seen progress or change, discuss this with him, and find out why nothing has happened. Remember: *Actions speak louder than words.*

MISTAKE **4** _____

Women Cover Up Their Excellence and Competence

Do you have a bad habit of putting yourself down in front of the man you love?

Do you have a difficult time receiving compliments and praise?

Do you possess talents and abilities your partner isn't even aware of?

Most women are so good at making Mistake #4 that they don't even know it. We cover up our intelligence, accomplishments, clarity, and abilities in order to avoid threatening the man in our life and to make him feel better about himself. We do this in several ways.

1. We talk about ourselves in derogatory terms, putting ourselves down for the slightest mistake, and therefore appearing not to like ourselves very much.

> "I can't believe how stupid I was to forget about your business meeting tonight. Sometimes I just can't seem to remember anything."

> "My boss said he was happy with my report, but I don't think I did a very good job. I got kind of confused about the financial projections and didn't really know what I was talking about."

> "I'm so upset about how fat I am getting. Would you look at this cellulite?"

2. We argue with men when they attempt to pay us a compliment and we act as if we want to talk them out of their positive opinion of us.

> "Really? You like this dress? Why, it's two years old. I really don't think the style is that flattering, but I wanted to get some wear out of it. Thanks anyway."

> "Oh, honey, planning the surprise party for you was really nothing. I mean, it didn't take that much time, and I had help. You don't have to make such a fuss over it."

> "You enjoyed my presentation? Well, actually, I felt kind of rushed since I was the last person to speak, and I wasn't sure if my facts would be well received. I think everyone was just relieved that the meeting was over—that's why I got all that applause."

3. We hide our talents and accomplishments from the men in our life.

Sondra was a perfect example of a woman who makes Mistake #4. She'd been married to Greg for seven years, and was an expert at making herself appear to be less competent and intelligent than he was. "Greg likes to feel like he's in charge," Sondra confided to me in a soft voice, "so I guess you could say I have always downplayed myself from the time we first started dating." Sondra was understating the facts—the truth was, she'd never even told Greg that she'd finished college with honors and had earned a scholarship to graduate school. He had no idea that she spoke fluent French, or that she'd been invited to work for a very successful French businessman in Paris before she'd met him. Sondra "neglected" to tell Greg these things about herself because, as she put it, "they're really not that important anymore."

Ellen, 37, and her husband, Andy, 39, were a two-career couple. Andy was an investment counselor for a large brokerage firm, and Ellen was in charge of public relations for a clothing manufacturer. They came to me for counseling after noticing some difficulties in their marriage. "I don't feel like Andy really appreciates me the way he should," Ellen complained. "I work as hard as he does, but we always seem to discuss his problems and not mine."

"It's true, we do spend more time talking about my job," Andy replied, "but I suppose that's because my work is more complex than yours." Naturally Ellen was furious when she heard her husband making his job the more important of the two.

I talked with Ellen and Andy for a while until I discovered the source of the problem. Ellen was making Mistake #4—constantly hiding her accomplishments from Andy and downplaying the importance of her work in order to make him feel more important. Of course, she wasn't doing this consciously. It was a habit she'd developed from growing up as the smarter, older sister to a younger brother, and always being told by her parents, "Now Ellen, don't you go telling Jonathan how well you did in school this semester—you know he's having trouble with his grades."

Ellen continued this same behavior with her husband.

She never let him know about the important clients she was assigned to meet and work with; she neglected to tell him how well respected she was by her peers; and she rarely shared her dreams and goals for the future with him. "No wonder I don't feel appreciated by Andy," Ellen admitted after hearing about Mistake #4. "I haven't been appreciating myself, and how could he even know how terrific I am if I hide it from him?"

There are millions of us like Ellen and Sandy—competent, talented, hard-working women who don't know how to celebrate their magnificence with the men in their lives.

Why We Cover Up Our Excellence and Competence

▼ **We cover up our excellence and competence because we think men will love us more that way.**

Do you remember ever being told any of the following things as a young girl?

> "Always let the boy win if you play games together. That way, he'll like you more."

> "Don't act too smart around men, or they won't want to take you out. You have to build them up, and make them feel smarter than you."

▼

AS WOMEN, WE'VE BEEN CONDITIONED TO MAKE OUR MEN LOOK AND FEEL SMARTER AND BETTER THAN WE ARE IN ORDER TO ENSURE THAT THEY WILL LOVE US

▲

We go into relationships with a belief that if we look too good to a man, he won't want to be with us, and so we work hard to make him look better than he is, and to make ourselves look worse than we are.

▼ **We cover up our excellence and competence because we're afraid to look arrogant or conceited to others.**

Do you remember being given advice like the following?

> "Now Susie, I'm glad that you got all A's on your report card, but I wouldn't tell too many people about it. It isn't nice to brag, and girls must be modest."

> "Ginny, don't stare at yourself in the mirror like that. It isn't ladylike to think too highly of yourself. Girls who are too proud are unpopular."

I remember my mother telling me when I was still in junior high school that the more successful and accomplished I became, the more people would be jealous of me, the less friends I'd have, and that I should be careful not to intimidate people with my talents. Like all mothers, she meant well, and I can't say that I haven't experienced some of these reactions in my life. But she was just passing down a self-deprecating philosophy that her mother had taught her, and that so many of us learned growing up. *A woman shouldn't look too good—it's not feminine or attractive.*

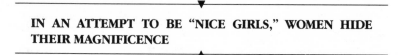

IN AN ATTEMPT TO BE "NICE GIRLS," WOMEN HIDE THEIR MAGNIFICENCE

Why Hiding Your Competence Doesn't Work

1. Hiding your competence kills the passion in your relationship. When we diminish our accomplishments and hide our excellence from the men in our lives, we think we're going to make ourselves less threatening and therefore more attractive to the man we love, but in reality, the opposite occurs:

▼

MEN ARE TURNED ON BY COMPETENCE AND TURNED OFF BY WEAKNESS

▲

Men love competence in women. They are trained to be competent themselves, and recognizing it in someone else makes them feel attracted to that person. During my research for this book, I interviewed hundreds of men, and almost all of them agreed that a woman who exudes self-confidence is very appealing. The men respect these women and take them more seriously.

Here's the irony—women think that hiding their magnificence and acting humble is going to get a man to love them more, when the truth is, this kind of behavior kills the passion in the relationship.

3. When you are in the habit of hiding your competence from men, you end up hiding it from yourself as well. The saying "out of sight, out of mind" definitely holds true for Mistake #4. The more you minimize your accomplishments to others, the less you remember them yourself, until eventually you lose touch with your own magnificence.

THE SOLUTION: HOW TO STOP COVERING UP YOUR COMPETENCE

1. Make a list of all of your talents, abilities, honors, accomplishments, and good qualities, and share this list with your partner. I've given this assignment to women in my seminars, and have heard some amazing stories about the results it produced. Many women report that just writing out their good qualities, abilities, and successes reminded them of things they'd completely forgotten and certainly never talked about with their partners. And the men report that they are surprised and delighted to discover more characteristics about their women to love.

2. Catch yourself not accepting compliments, putting yourself down, or minimizing your achievements, and practice CELEBRATING YOUR MAGNIFICENCE. You'll be surprised to notice how often you make Mistake #4, and how much of an unconscious habit it's become. Catch yourself in the act, and shift from covering up your excellence to celebrating yourself. The next time someone compliments you, take a deep breath and simply say, "Thank you!" Throw your false modesty out the window.

3. Look for a man who wants to let you shine. We all know there are men out there who, for a variety of reasons, don't want to be with a woman who appears powerful or confident. It's hard to celebrate yourself around someone who isn't interested in seeing you shine. Make sure your partner supports you in becoming the magnificent woman you're meant to be.

MISTAKE **5**

Women Give Up Their Power to Men

I'm sad to say that the phrase "women give up their power to men" is, for many of us, redundant. As we've seen so far, throughout history a woman's role has been to give her power away to a man, so it's been more of an unfortunate fact of life than a mistake. I can tell you from experience that discovering how you give your power away to the men in your life, and learning how to stop doing it, will be one of the most important steps you can take toward creating healthy, loving relationships.

I have a name for those of us who give our power away to men, hoping they will love us more because of it: Love

Martyrs. A martyr is a person who decides to make a personal sacrifice for a cause. In the case of women, we often sacrifice our self-respect, our sense of personal dignity and integrity, and our self-esteem in order to get a man to love us.

Are You a Love Martyr?

Here's a quiz that will help you determine how serious a Love Martyr you are. It contains ten warning signs of a Love Martyr. You can take this quiz based on the relationship you are in now, one from the past, or your relationships with men in general. Grade yourself on each statement according to how frequently that statement applies to you.

Very frequently	0 points
Often	4 points
Occasionally	8 points
Rarely or never	10 points

Answer as honestly as you can. You may not like admitting some of this to yourself, but facing it is the first step toward changing it.

The Ten Warning Signs of a Love Martyr

1. You feel like you have to tiptoe around your partner to avoid upsetting or displeasing him.
2. You feel that your partner doesn't always treat you with respect.
3. You act like a more confident, powerful person at work or with friends than you do around your partner.
4. You don't feel safe or comfortable giving negative feedback to your partner.
5. You're hesitant to ask your partner for what you want and need, and sometimes wonder if you are too "needy" or "insecure" anyway.

6. You feel that your partner treats you worse than you treat him.

7. When your partner isn't behaving lovingly toward you, you tend to become more loving toward him in hopes of winning him over.

8. You feel you have to work to convince your partner of your rights for love, affection, equality, freedom, etc.

9. You often defend or make excuses, to yourself or others, for your partner's behavior or your life situation.

10. You often feel angry at yourself for acting like a "wimp" around a man, but even though you vow never to do it again, you continue to allow yourself to be treated less lovingly than you deserve.

Now, total up your points.

80–100 points: Congratulations! You own your power around the men in your life, and usually don't sacrifice who you are in order to be loved. To avoid future problems, work on those areas in which you had a lower score.

60–79 points: You're not a full-blown Love Martyr, but you are giving up your power too often in certain areas of your relationships with men. Notice how you are letting fear of loss or disapproval keep you from asking for what you deserve from your partner. Work on loving yourself more and compromising less.

40–59 points: WARNING! Whether you want to admit it or not, you are a wimp when it comes to your relationships with men. You allow yourself to be treated badly, and don't stick up for yourself. You're such an expert at sacrificing for love that you've forgotten how it feels to be relaxed around a man. Follow the instructions in this chapter carefully, and start giving yourself some of the love you give so easily to men.

0–39 points: EMERGENCY! YOU'RE A PROFESSIONAL LOVE MARTYR. You probably have little or no self-respect left, considering how terribly you're treated by the men in your life. Don't expect to be loved until you start loving yourself. It's time to get off the floor and act like a woman, and not a doormat! You need to take action NOW! Use the suggestions in this book, seek some personal counseling for extra support, stop sacrificing and start living with dignity again.

How We Don't Maintain Our Dignity As Women

All of these warning signs add up to the same thing: *not maintaining your dignity as a woman.* That means:

▼ Allowing yourself to be treated in ways you wouldn't want your daughter to be treated by a man

▼ Not sticking up for yourself when you know you should

▼ Living in fear of criticism or disapproval from your partner

▼ Settling for less than the amount of love and caring you know you deserve.

EACH TIME YOU GIVE YOUR POWER AWAY TO A MAN BY ALLOWING HIM TO TREAT YOU DISRESPECTFULLY OR UNLOVINGLY, YOU LOSE RESPECT AND LOVE FOR YOURSELF

This creates what I call a Negative Self-Esteem Cycle. Here's how it works: You allow a man to get away with mistreating you—maybe he calls you names, or refuses to comfort you when you're upset, or acts like an angry child when you try to talk about the relationship, or is insensitive to your feelings in some way. You don't stick up for yourself, and this results in your feeling upset, depressed, and bad about yourself.

When you feel bad about yourself, your self-confidence decreases. And when your self-confidence is low, the next time that man mistreats you, you will have even less courage to stand up for yourself, and the cycle repeats itself over and over.

The Negative Self-Esteem Cycle

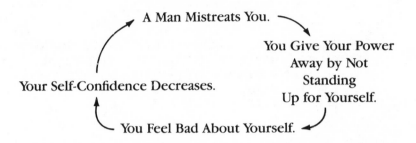

A Man Mistreats You.

You Give Your Power Away by Not Standing Up for Yourself.

Your Self-Confidence Decreases.

You Feel Bad About Yourself.

There is only one way to break this endless cycle: Stand up for yourself and maintain your dignity; do not allow yourself to be treated with less love and respect than you know you deserve. When you do this, you feel good about yourself, and in turn, your self-confidence increases. The next time you aren't treated well, *you will own your power rather than giving it away.*

ARE YOU COMFORTABLE WITH BEING MISTREATED BY MEN?

Have you ever bought a new car, driven it for the first time, and suddenly realized how difficult your old car was to drive?

Have you ever moved from one apartment or home to another, more spacious one, and suddenly realized how cramped your old place was?

Have you ever put on a new, comfortable pair of shoes and suddenly realized how uncomfortable the old pair was?

Whether you know it or not, you may be giving your power away to men and allowing yourself to be treated poorly in relationships because you are used to being treated that way. As human beings we tend to become comfortable where we are, and often don't realize the shortcomings of our situation until we are in a new one. All at once, we feel the contrast between the two pairs of shoes, or apartments, or cars, or relationships, and then we can admit to ourselves that we were uncomfortable before.

▼

AS WOMEN WE ARE SO ACCUSTOMED TO *NOT* BEING TREATED WITH RESPECT AND DIGNITY THAT WE ALLOW MEN TO LOVE US MUCH LESS THAN WE DESERVE TO BE LOVED

▲

Until recently, I had given my power away to every man I've been in a relationship with. I allowed myself to be unappreciated; I put up with behavior that I would never allow one of my clients to tolerate from her partner; I sacrificed what I wanted and needed in order to accommodate my mate; I lived in constant fear of disapproval. Was I aware that I was being a Love Martyr? No! I would have sworn that I was behaving as a powerful, self-confident woman. The truth was, I was so comfortable and familiar with giving my power away that I didn't even know I was doing it. Were the men in my life to blame? Not at all! I didn't act lovingly toward myself, and they just followed suit.

Now, for the first time in my life, I'm learning to maintain my dignity in a relationship with a man, and it's not easy! That habit of being a Love Martyr still tries to creep back in and get me to sacrifice anything for love. But with the help of the techniques in this book, the support of my female friends, and the encouragement of the man in my life who wants me to own my power (and can't stand when I act like a wimp!), I am becoming the powerful woman in my relationships that I worked so hard to be in my career.

FROM WIMP TO BITCH: HOW WOMEN TIPTOE AROUND MEN AND
THEN REBEL AGAINST THEM

Louis, 36, and Linda, 32, had been dating for nine months
when they came to see me for counseling. "Linda is driving
me crazy," Louis began. "When I met her, I thought she was
really sweet and loving, the kind of woman I could spend my
life with. But after two or three months, she seemed to
change completely. She became defensive, sarcastic, even
cold at times. I've tried to talk to her about this, but she just
tells me that this is the way she is, and to stop trying to
change her. I hate to admit it, but I feel like she's turned into
a real bitch."

As Louis told his story, Linda sat on the couch with a
very hard look on her face. Something told me I'd have a
better chance of getting through to her without Louis in the
room, so I asked him to leave.

"Tell me about yourself, Linda," I asked. "I'd like to hear
about your relationships before Louis."

"I was engaged to a guy for two years when I was
twenty-nine," Linda answered. "I was crazy about him, and
would have done anything to make him happy. In fact, that's
how I got to California. He was transferred here from Texas,
and so I quit my job and moved here to be with him. He was
seven years older than me, and I guess I had him on a
pedestal."

As Linda spoke about her ex-fiancé, her eyes filled with
tears and her face began to soften. "What happened between
you?" I asked gently.

"I was so stupid," she blurted out. "He never treated me
well, but I just took it. I put up with such shit from him. And
he kept putting off setting a wedding date. One day I came
home early from work and found him in bed with some
secretary he'd met at his office. Do you know that he even
tried to convince me that his screwing her meant nothing,
and that there wasn't any reason to break off the
engagement?"

I held Linda in my arms as she sobbed her heart out, and I understood her relationship with Louis. Linda had spent so many years giving up her power to her fiancé, and being so hurt that she'd unconsciously decided to go to the other extreme and never let a man affect her again. She'd swung from wimp to bitch—from tiptoeing around her fiancé to rebelling against Louis. No wonder Louis couldn't understand the personality change in Linda.

Many women go through this same pattern in their lives. They have a relationship in which they give up their power and act like a wimp, and then, vowing never to do that again, they rebel by acting like a bitch with the next, unsuspecting man they fall in love with. Then they realize that doesn't work, and go back to being a wimp again. And on and on.

Another variation on this theme occurs when we swing from wimp to bitch in the same relationship. I have a friend who drives her husband crazy with this pattern. She acts submissive and wimpy around him for a week or so, then gets really angry at herself for being so weak, and swings in the other direction, acting cold and distant. He gets fed up with her coldness and confronts her, she breaks down and apologizes and goes back to being wimpy.

This is the kind of behavior that tempts men to call women "moody," "unpredictable," "temperamental," and "infuriating." The answer is to find a balance somewhere between wimp and bitch, to live in integrity with our own values so we can free ourselves from the cycle of submission and rebellion.

THE SOLUTION: HOW TO STOP GIVING YOUR POWER AWAY TO MEN

Here are some suggestions to help you combat Mistake #5:

1. Stop rewarding the men in your life for mistreating you. Veronica and her husband David just had a terrible argument. It all started when Veronica asked David to help her choose some new wallpaper for their kitchen, and David expressed no interest in it. The more Veronica asked, the more upset David grew, until he became furious, yelled at Veronica, calling her a "controlling bitch," and stormed out of the house.

Now Veronica is lying on her bed sobbing, wishing she could turn the clock back a few hours before the fight. She hears David come back in the house, go into the den, and turn on the TV. Anxious to make up, and desperate to feel close to her husband again, Veronica walks into the den, kneels down by David's chair, puts her head on his lap and sniffles a little while he watches his program. After a few minutes, she feels David's hand reach out and stroke her hair, and knows that he's not angry anymore. Veronica turns around, reaches out her arms to David and says, "Oh, honey, I'm so glad you're back. I missed you. I don't want to fight with you." "I don't want to fight with you either," David says with a sigh of relief. The couple kiss, and settle in for a cozy evening together.

Sharon and her boyfriend Ernie are standing in the middle of their apartment having a huge fight. Ernie just finished informing Sharon that he's having dinner with an ex-lover, one who doesn't know he is living with Sharon. When Sharon asks Ernie if he's told his ex about her, he admits that he hasn't, but insists that it's because this girl is emotionally unstable, and he doesn't want to hurt her feelings. Sharon is enraged that Ernie isn't being honest about their relationship. "You're more interested in how your stupid ex-girlfriend feels than how I feel!" she accuses Ernie. "I don't need to hear this shit," Ernie yells, and slamming the door beind him, leaves for work.

All day, Sharon feels miserable thinking about Ernie and his ex having dinner, and about how insensitive he was to her that morning. As the hours pass, her fears intensify, until all she can think about is losing Ernie. She knows she won't

see Ernie until late that night, and decides to plan a big
surprise for him when he returns. She bakes his favorite cake,
buys a bottle of good wine, and decorates their apartment
with candles. At 11:30 Ernie returns, and Sharon races to the
door and into his arms. "Welcome home, darling," she
whispers. "I missed you. I never want to lose you." "I don't
want to lose you either," Ernie replies, relieved that Sharon
is in such a good mood. And they have a wonderful evening
together.

What did you think when you read these two stories?
Did you feel like these were happy endings? Did you feel that
the two women knew how to handle their men well? If you
did, you were *Wrong*! Veronica and Sharon may have believed
they were being understanding, loving, and forgiving, but
they were really being Love Martyrs at their worst: They
were rewarding their partners for mistreating them!

▼

ONE OF THE BIGGEST MISTAKES WOMEN MAKE WITH MEN IS REWARDING THEM WITH LOVING BEHAVIOR AFTER THEY'VE TREATED US BADLY

▲

How do we do this? We hug and kiss a man who is saying
disrespectful things to us; we don't talk back to a man who is
yelling at us, and then we apologize for getting him angry;
we make love to a man who just a few moments or hours
before treated us like dirt, and still hasn't said he was sorry;
we pamper and fuss over a man who has done something to
hurt our feelings, to show him that we still love him.

What's the message men get when we act this way?
*You can treat me any way you want. I still love you. In fact,
the worse you treat me, the more frightened I will become,
and the more loving I will be.*

The equivalent of this would be this: You have a little
dog, and you have a nice, new white couch, and you come
home one day to find that your dog made doo-doo all over

the white couch, and you go in the kitchen, get some doggie treats and give them to your dog as a reward! This is what a kiss to a man who's being mean to you says.

Animal trainers always stress the importance of disciplining your dog—you take his nose and push it in the doo-doo, and you whack him on the nose with a newspaper so that he gets the message: Don't make doo-doo on the couch again, or else. Now, I'm not suggesting that when your man "misbehaves," you roll up a newspaper and whack away. I am saying that rewarding a man for mistreating you trains him to continue that behavior.

What should you do when a man treats you in a way that is unacceptable?

▼ Communicate your hurt and angry feelings to him.

▼ Wait to hear a response that indicates he understands how you feel, and feels remorse for his behavior.

▼ Discuss ways you can both deal with the situation with more wisdom and sensitivity the next time it comes up.

▼ Then, kiss and make up!

2. Make two lists: The ways I give up my power to men. The ways I give up my power in my relationship.
This is an important process to do on paper. Writing down each of the ways you act like a Love Martyr will help make you more conscious of these behaviors, and is the first step toward changing them. Share these lists with a girlfriend when you're done, as a way to commit yourself not to give away your power anymore.

3. Make a list of rules for yourself about healthy behaviors you can engage in and "no-no" behaviors you want to avoid around men. I'll explain more about how to create a rulebook in the final chapter.

4. Maintain Your Dignity. I love this phrase. I write it on little pieces of paper and stick them all over the place as a reminder of who I really am. Sometimes, when I find myself in the middle of Love Martyr behavior, I close my eyes and just meditate on this phrase and what it means for a few moments. It almost always brings me back to a centered place of self-respect. You'll know what this phrase means to you, and how you need to maintain your dignity as a woman.

▼

REMEMBER: OWNING YOUR POWER WITH MEN DOES *NOT* MEAN HAVING POWER OVER THEM, BUT *EMPOW-ERING YOURSELF* BY TREATING YOURSELF WITH LOVE AND RESPECT, AND MAKING SURE THE MEN IN YOUR LIFE DO THE SAME

▲

MISTAKE **6**

Women Act Like Little Girls to Get What They Want from Men

When you were a little girl, you got a lot of attention for being sweet, cute, and vulnerable. You may not realize how often you still do this around men, especially when you want love and appreciation. I feel so sad when I watch women make Mistake #6, and I feel even worse when I see how men just eat this behavior up.

How do you do this?

1. Acting naive or ignorant when you know the truth or the answer. This makes men feel smart and that they know what they are doing. It gives them a false sense of self-esteem, and allows them to feel comfortable around you only because they feel superior, and not because they respect you.

2. Acting hurt when you're really angry.

Do you ever cry when you're actually pissed off?

Do you ever pout when you really need to tell a man he's acting like an asshole and you're fed up?

Do you ever sulk instead of getting up and leaving?

Since most of us were taught that it's not nice for girls to get angry, we suppress our angry emotions and express the more acceptable "female" feelings, such as sadness, fear, and guilt, thus leaving the anger to smolder and stagnate inside of us. We do this because it is much less threatening, and therefore more lovable, to men.

3. Pretending to be confused when you are not. This is one of our worst habits as women—we pretend we don't know what we want or how we feel, or what to do. We make ourselves look mentally helpless, and then here comes a man to our rescue. Surprise, surprise! He feels so competent, so helpful.

We use confusion as a cover-up for other grown-up, more unpleasant emotions, such as anger, resentment, guilt, hurt, and fear. I can't even count how many times I've counseled women who've said things like, "I'm so confused about my relationship, I don't know what's happening." And when I ask them to explain more, they respond, "Well, my husband is cheating on me, we haven't had sex in two years, I feel worthless, but I'm so confused." Of course, there's nothing confusing about this situation at all, but if this woman acts confused, then she doesn't have to make any decisions or take responsibility for how her life turns out.

4. Treating men like Daddy

There's nothing wrong with allowing the man you love to take care of you once in a while in a fatherly way, but your relationship is in trouble if you treat him like a father figure much of the time. This includes such habits as

▼ actually calling your lover "Daddy"

▼ sitting on his lap and pouting

▼ confessing to him that you've "been a bad girl" that day

▼ letting your husband control all of the money and give you an "allowance"

I won't go into the more serious psychological connotations of this kind of behavior. It's enough to say that the more you set the man in your life up as Daddy, the more you remain a child.

5. Speaking to a man in a whiny, little-girl voice rather than as a woman.
As women, we resort to using our little girl voice especially when:

▼ We're afraid to say what is on our mind.

▼ We're frightened of the man's reaction.

▼ We expect disagreement.

Talking like a little girl says to a man, "Look, I'm just a little girl. Don't hurt me, and don't be mean to me, okay?"

6. Creating chaos in your life so that you can get a man to rescue you.

▼ Do you live from one crisis to the next?

▼ Is there always something urgent you need a man's help or advice with?

▼ Do you secretly enjoy being rescued?

Part of the little-girl game is setting yourself up to fall apart, so a man can come along and rescue you. Maybe you do this because Daddy was never there for you in your real life. Maybe you do this to "test" your man, to see if you can depend on him. The problem is that it keeps you addicted to crisis as a way to get attention—a definite little-girl tactic.

HOW ACTING LIKE A LITTLE GIRL AFFECTS THE MEN IN YOUR LIFE

Men won't respect you. Will men respond to the little-girl routine? Absolutely. It makes them feel big and strong and in charge. They'll probably get sucked into it. They may even enjoy it. But they won't respect you, and will end up treating you like a little girl, and not like the woman you are. That means less passion and less real love.

Men will resent you. When you behave like a little girl, it makes men feel responsible for you. As we'll see throughout the book, men already feel overwhelmed by responsibility in life. So even though a man might respond to your helplessness by rescuing you, he probably will end up feeling tremendous resentment about it in the end.

THE SOLUTION: HOW TO STOP ACTING LIKE A LITTLE GIRL AROUND MEN

1. Make a list: "The Ways I Play Little Girl Around Men." This might be embarrassing, even humiliating to do, but believe me, it will help cure you of Mistake Number Six. The next time you catch yourself twirling your hair around your finger, or talking in a sing-song voice, or whatever your habits are, you'll become disgusted with yourself and stop.

2. When you find yourself crying, ask yourself: "Is there something I'm angry about?" This is important to remember, especially if you know you have a difficult time feeling and expressing anger. You may find that even though you are crying, you're actually really mad. Then you can choose to communicate your real feelings like an adult, rather than hiding them beneath tears. Of course, this doesn't mean you shouldn't let yourself cry, or that you are always mad when you weep. It's just something to be on the lookout for.

3. The next time you feel helpless or confused, ask yourself: "If I weren't confused, I might feel . . ." This is a terrific exercise for clearing out confusion. Before you collapse into confusion and expect some man to rescue you, see if you can get clear on your own. Some of your little-girl habits are probably very old, and giving them up won't be easy. But it will feel wonderful to be loved and appreciated for the woman in you.

I hope I've helped you understand a little more about your relationships with men by sharing these Six Mistakes. I'm sure that by now you realize that I didn't come up with this list by doing research in psychological journals or taking a survey, but by making every one of those Six Mistakes myself over and over again! Like most women, I've done all the wrong things to try to get a man to love me, and I've had to learn the hard way. Perhaps you'll have an easier time now that you know some pitfalls to watch out for and some techniques to practice.

It's hard to break old habits, no matter how much we want to. In the next few days and weeks, you'll catch yourself doing many of the things that you just read about. When that happens, *don't be discouraged. Remember: the first step in changing yourself is always to become aware of things you're doing that are hurting you.* So memorize these Six Mistakes, do all the exercises, share this information with your friends, and get the support you need to become the powerful, loving woman you know you want to be.

3 | Filling in the Emotional Blanks: How to Stop Giving More Than You Get in Love

"I give and I give, and he loves me for it, but sometimes I wonder if he would love me as much if I stopped giving all the time."

▼

"I've always been the one who loves more in my relationships. My fantasy is to find a man who gives as much to me as I give to him, but I don't think men like that really exist."

▼

"I feel like I'm the one who's holding up the emotional end of our relationship—that if I stopped working so hard to keep it together, my husband wouldn't know what to do, and our marriage would just fall apart."

Have you ever felt the way these women feel—that you give more than you get in relationships? Have you ever secretly wished that you could be loved by a man as much as you love him? This chapter is about the biggest mistake women make in relationships—how we as women love men more than they love us back. I decided to devote an entire chapter to this mistake rather than include it with the Six Mistakes, because I feel this pattern is too important to be talked about lightly.

This was the hardest and most painful chapter for me to write, because it hit so close to home. I was to begin writing this chapter on a Friday, and when I went to sleep Thursday night, I had one nightmare after another—dark, confusing dreams full of fear, sadness, and loss. When I woke up in the morning, I wasn't sure why I'd had such a disturbing night— that is, until I sat down at my computer, typed out the title of this chapter, and burst into tears. As I stared at the words before me with tears streaming down my face. I suddenly knew what had caused those nightmares, and what was causing me to weep right now: It was the pain of my own broken heart, the pain that comes from having given so much more in love, so many times in my life, than I was given back; the pain that comes from years spent trying to make relation- ships work, and realizing that my partner wasn't willing to try as hard as I was; the pain that came from being an expert at loving another person, and not knowing how to love myself.

The tears I cried that day were not just for me and my pain, but for yours as well. I know firsthand that many of you walk around with that same broken heart that comes from not being loved enough. I can't even count how many times I've sat and listened to a woman weep as she described her relationship with her husband or her boyfriend, and seen her look at me with such pain in her eyes and ask, "I just don't understand . . . I love him so much. I give him everything I can, and he still doesn't love me the way I know I love him. What am I doing wrong?" And each time I give one of my Making Love Work seminars, some woman stands up, turns to her husband with tears in her eyes, and says, "Honey, you know how much I adore you. But it's just breaking my heart to feel that I have to keep begging you to show me you love me, that you don't just give it to me like I give my love to you."

The Most Lovable Little Girl in the World

There once was a little girl who, more than anything in the whole world, wanted to live happily ever after. She read fairy tales about princesses and princes and true love, and decided that when she grew up, she would search and search until she found the kind of relationship the books described. She figured she'd better start preparing for her romantic destiny right away. When she looked around for Prince Charming types, the only one she could find was her daddy. Like most young girls, she thought her daddy was perfect, and cherished his love. And so it was natural that her father became the man in her life who she could count on to make her happy.

One day, the little girl's father packed his bags and told her he was moving away. He explained that even though he still loved her very much, he couldn't live with her mother anymore, and had to leave. The little girl ran upstairs to her room, threw herself down on the bed and wept. *How can he leave me?* she cried to herself. *If he really loved me, he would stay. I must not be lovable enough.* And in that moment, the little girl vowed that she would become so lovable, and would love her daddy so well, that he would come back to her.

So the little girl set out to become the most lovable little girl on earth. She figured out what she had to do to make her daddy happy, and did all of those things—she got all A's in school; she tried out for plays and learned to act; she read lots and lots of books. But most of all, she worked hard at proving to her daddy that she thought he was wonderful, because she discovered that, more than anything, her daddy would love her when he felt loved. She would listen attentively to his stories and laugh at the funny parts and get frightened at the scary parts; she would tell her daddy that he was the smartest, most handsome man in the world. And she would never, never disagree with him or criticize him because she knew that if she did, he wouldn't love her very much at those times.

Well, the little girl's daddy never did move back into the house. But he did love her very much, he treated her as his favorite child, so she decided that her plan had worked! Even her daddy agreed, telling her, "You are the most loving little girl in the world." Now she was ready for the big time.

How to Seduce a Seventh-Grade Prince

The girl grew up, and when it was time for her to fall in love, she felt confident that she knew just what to do. "The secret," she'd confide to her girlfriends in junior high school, "is to love your boyfriend so-o-o-o-o much, and be so-o-o-o-o wonderful, and make him feel so-o-o-o-o good, that he can't live without you." And that's just what she did. She found a boy she liked, and started to love him. She left him notes in his locker every day, and cheered for him at every basketball practice, and always made sure to tell him how perfectly wonderful he was. And she loved him and loved him and loved him until he said to himself, *Wow, no one has ever loved me like this before, not even my own parents. I guess I'm in love with her.*

For a while, the girl was happy. *This is my prince,* she'd tell herself, *and I am his princess.* But after some time, she began to notice that even though she had a boyfriend, she wasn't happy. And she realized that although she was treating him like a prince, he was definitely *not* treating her like a princess. And she would run to her room, throw herself down on the bed and weep, thinking, *I love him more than he loves me. How can this be happening when I'm giving him so much?* And she couldn't figure out the answer.

THE QUEEN OF HEARTS

The years passed, the girl grew into a woman, the boys were now men, and the crushes were now love affairs or marriages. And though the details of the story changed, the plot remained the same: she desperately tried to keep her man by working hard at being totally loving and lovable. Now instead of leaving notes in lockers and giving compliments in the school hallways, the woman armed herself with more serious ammunition: she would overwhelm the man in her life with love poems, short stories, and clever cards; she supplied a steady stream of gifts and surprises; she made herself indispensable with her helpful advice and wise counsel; she would lavish her lover with praise, affection, and sexual attention until he felt like the most loved man on earth.

And each time, with each man, the same thing would happen. He would tell her how wonderful she was, that no one had ever loved him as much as she did, that she was the Queen of Hearts, and he was a lucky man to have her. And she would be so busy giving that she never stopped to ask herself if she was being given to, until one day she would notice that her man was doing a good job of taking from her, but not a very good job of giving back. And that when she stopped always being the one to reach out, he wouldn't reach back. And that even though he was there with her, she felt very much alone.

And soon, the man would admit, "I guess I don't love you as much as you love me," and they would say good-bye. And the woman would run to her bedroom, throw herself on the bed and weep, thinking, *How can this happen to me over and over again? I've worked so hard at being the most loving woman on earth. Why can't I find a man to love me back as much as I love him?* And after all those years crying on all those beds, she still couldn't figure out the answer.

Working Hard for Love

The woman I've been writing about isn't a client, or someone who attended one of my seminars. That woman is me, and her story is the story of my life. I was the little girl who decided I had to earn a man's love. I was the teenager who learned to overwhelm a boy with attention and appreciation until he convinced himself that he was in love with me. And I was the woman who, until recently, worked so hard at constantly giving to the men in my life that I never stopped to notice I wasn't getting back what I needed.

Like so many of you, I thought that I had to *do* something in order to get a man to love me. I became a professional giver. And unfortunately, I was so good at it that it worked— I would give a man so much, he'd think he was in love with me, when in reality he was in love with what I was giving him.

No wonder I never felt really loved by a man. No wonder my relationships left me feeling ripped off and betrayed, even when I was the one who did the leaving. Here were the results in my life:

▼ **I ended up with the "wrong men."** I was so busy worrying about how much the man loved me that I didn't stop and ask myself how much I loved him.

I was so busy worrying about if the man thought I was the right woman for him that I didn't stop and ask myself if he was the right man for me.

Therefore, I'd have relationships with men I loved but I didn't like, or wasn't compatible with, i.e.—the "wrong men," because I didn't pay attention to how I felt about them.

▼ **I didn't give men a chance to find out how they really felt about me.** I was so busy "selling myself" to the man I loved that I never created the space for him to want me *on his own*. That abandoned little girl inside me didn't trust that a man would want to stay with me just for being me, so she worked like hell to make herself appear so valuable to a man that he'd feel he needed her in his life and couldn't live without her.

How Women Fill in the Emotional Blanks

I call what I used to do, and what so many women do, "filling in the emotional blanks" in a relationship. We have a picture in our mind of what we think a good relationship should look like, and we find a man and go about creating that relationship without much participation on his part. It's as if we say to him, "You show up every day, and I'll take care of the emotional part of the relationship. I'll create the intimacy, the social activities, the conversations, and the direction. All you have to do is agree to be my partner." The danger in doing this is that we often end up practically having a relationship with ourselves. We work so hard to make the relationship look good that we get tricked into believing it's a mutual creation, when in reality it's a solo performance and the man has a front-row seat.

Here is a list of some of the ways women fill in the emotional blanks. You may relate to one or all of them.

1. Filling in the social and activity blanks. You're the one who thinks of and plans most of your social activities:

> You read the paper, notice what shows or events are in town, and convince your partner to go.
> You make suggestions to your partner about how to spend your weekends.
> You think ahead to next week or next month and schedule activities.
> You are the one who plans holidays and special occasions.
> You make most of the phone calls to friends and relatives (even his) and arrange visits and get-togethers.
> You suggest new and interesting things to do and try— new restaurants and the like.

You initiate discussion about and plan the details of vacations.

2. Filling in the sexual blanks. You're the one who initiates most of the sexual and physical contact:

You're the one to reach out and give a hug or ask for one first.

You usually grab your partner's hand first in movie theaters, or walking down the street, or watching TV.

You initiate kissing most of the time.

You move over to stand near your partner from wherever you are in a room.

You're the one to make the first sexual advances toward your partner, or complain that you're not making love enough. (Note: This might be the only one in this category that the man does.)

You move from your side of the bed to your partner's side of the bed at night to cuddle before you go to sleep.

3. Filling in the intimacy blanks. You're the one who initiates most of the intimacy in the relationship:

You remind your partner that it's been awhile since you had romantic time together.

You're the one who suggests you talk about your feelings together.

You're the one who brings up the topic of commitment, or the future.

You create the environment for intimacy—music, candles, special evenings.

You leave most of the notes, give most of the cards or little gifts, write most of the letters.

You're the one who usually approaches your partner first to make up after a fight.

4. Filling in the communication blanks. You're the one who initiates most of the communication in the relationship:

> You talk more than your partner when you are together.
> You ask more questions of your partner than he does of you.
> You feel nervous when your partner is silent for long periods, and probe by asking how he is feeling or what he is thinking.
> When you don't get a response from your partner to what you are saying, you suggest things he might be feeling as a way to carry on both sides of the conversation.
> You find yourself trying to figure out what your partner is feeling or second-guess him since he doesn't volunteer information.
> You make suggestions as to how your partner should talk to his boss, an employee, his mother, or your kids, and tell him what he should say.

5. Filling in the creative blanks. You're the one who contributes most of the creativity to the relationship:

> You bring up most of the new ideas or concepts to discuss.
> You suggest more ways to change things—your relationship, your habits, or your room decorations.
> You introduce your partner to new music, new books, new foods.

We all initiate these activities some of the time. However, if you are the one in the relationship who *usually* does these things, you are definitely filling in the blanks.

How Filling in the Blanks Can Destroy Your Relationship

▼ **You build up resentment.** When you start out a relationship by filling in the blanks, you feel happy because you're "winning" your partner's love and all your hard work is paying off. Eventually, however, you begin to feel very resentful toward your partner when you realize that you're the one carrying the emotional load in the relationship.

Suzanne and Jerry were in a marital crisis when they came to see me. "I feel like I have to do everything in our relationship," Suzanne complained. "I make all of our plans, I call our friends, I suggest we talk about our problems. We've been married for seven years, and during that whole time, I don't think Jerry's ever taken charge."

Jerry appeared surprised to hear his wife's anger. "I always thought you loved doing all that stuff," he explained. "Ever since we dated, you were the one who was always planning our weekends and holidays. I guess I just got used to it and assumed you liked being in charge."

I worked with Suzanne and Jerry and helped them see the pattern they had fallen into: Suzanne was resentful because she didn't feel taken care of, and Jerry couldn't understand why, all of a sudden, she seemed angry about doing the things she'd always loved doing for him. The same tactics Suzanne used to get Jerry to love her were now backfiring, as she felt trapped in her role as the one responsible for the relationship.

▼ **You don't leave your partner any room to fill in the blanks himself.** When you are in the habit of filling in the blanks, you don't give your partner the opportunity to make the move to do it first. You become frustrated that your partner isn't taking charge more, not realizing that you aren't giving him a chance!

▼

MEN FEEL GOOD ABOUT THEMSELVES WHEN THEY TAKE CHARGE OR INITIATE ACTION, SO WHEN YOU DON'T GIVE THEM A CHANCE TO DO THIS, THEY WILL FEEL EMASCULATED AND RESENTFUL

▲

Eileen and Roy were caught in this dilemma. They'd been living together for three years when they came to my seminar. "I really love Roy," Eileen began, "but we have a big problem with sex. I don't feel that Roy is really attracted to me. I seem to be the one who always initiates sex, or who goes over to give him a hug or a kiss. When we do make love, it's great, but I wish he would be more aggressive with me."

"It's true," Roy agreed. "I guess I'm not that aggressive with Eileen. When I think about it, I feel like she just doesn't give me a chance. She's always coming on to me, telling me she wants me, grabbing me in the kitchen or when I come home from work. The truth is, I don't even think about approaching her—I don't have to. I know she's going to be putting her arms around me, or trying to seduce me, so I've gotten lazy about it."

Eileen didn't give Roy a chance to want her. The moment she felt any kind of gap in their sexual connection, she would rush in and fill in the blanks. He ended up feeling emasculated, she ended up feeling unloved, and they both felt resentful.

Like Roy, many men will react with ambivalent feelings when their partner is an expert at filling in the blanks. On the one hand, they feel relieved of the responsibility of having to consistently contribute to the relationship; on the other hand, they secretly feel ripped off of the opportunity to fill in the blanks themselves.

▼

WHEN YOU FILL IN THE BLANKS ALL THE TIME IN YOUR RELATIONSHIP, YOU DENY YOUR MAN THE OPPORTUNITY TO LEARN MORE ABOUT LOVING, AND THEREFORE, YOU DENY HIM THE OPPORTUNITY TO GROW

▲

▼ **You run the risk of deluding yourself into believing you have a good relationship.** When you are really an expert at filling in the blanks, you can create the illusion of a great relationship where there really isn't one. I'm sorry to say that I've done this several times in my life. Let me tell you about a relationship I had with a man I'll call Sandy. When I met Sandy, I knew he liked me, but I decided we were going to have a fabulous romance together. I began filling in the blanks of the relationship. I planned wonderful dates for us; I wrote Sandy beautiful poems and letters revealing my most vulnerable and private self; I'd bring up deep and philosophical topics of conversation, tell him my views on various subjects, and talk for hours. I'd inform him of my latest revelations about our relationship and what I was learning from it. And of course, I tried to get him into bed with me as much as possible!

Now, did Sandy resist any of my attempts to fill in the blanks? Absolutely not. On the contrary, he loved it. It helped him avoid those areas of his life where he felt inadequate, and it appealed to his ego to have a woman so crazy about him.

So here we were in this dynamic relationship. I'd describe it to my friends, and they all thought it sounded terrific. People who saw us together thought we looked really happy. And when I'd ask myself, *Do we have a good relationship?* I'd think about the exciting trip we'd just taken to Palm Springs, or the great lovemaking we'd had last week, or the lovely moment of intimacy we experienced when I gave him a poem I'd written. And I'd reassure myself, *Yes, we do have a great relationship.*

And then one day, Sandy walked in and told me he was leaving me. He explained that he hadn't been feeling really present in the relationship for a while, and didn't want to lead me on any longer. As I listened, I went into total shock. How could this be happening when our relationship had seemed so wonderful? Over the next few weeks, I looked at truths about myself that I hadn't wanted to face, and I found the answer to my question: My relationship with Sandy was basically a one-person show, starring me, with Sandy as a spectator. I was so busy filling in the blanks and creating the form of the relationship that I never stopped to examine the substance. The outside of our relationship had looked perfect—trips and cards and fun times. But the inside of the relationship was missing something essential: Sandy's participation and emotional investment.

Are You the One Rowing the Boat in Your Relationship?

Here's an analogy to help illustrate filling in the blanks in a relationship. Imagine you and your partner are in a rowboat on a lake. You are sitting in the front, and your partner is sitting in the back. You each have a pair of oars, and you assume you are both rowing, because the boat is moving nicely across the lake. *What a beautiful ride,* you think to yourself. *Don't we row well together.* At some point, you feel a little tired, and decide to stop rowing and rest for a while. All of a sudden the boat stops, and when you turn around to see what happened, you find your partner has just been sitting there all along, or has been asleep, letting you do all the rowing. He's been a passenger in the boat. Or perhaps, when you turn around, there isn't even anyone else in the boat—you've been alone the whole time.

▼

WHEN YOU WORK TO FILL IN THE EMOTIONAL BLANKS, YOUR PARTNER BECOMES A PASSENGER IN THE RELATIONSHIP

▲

In my own life, I was always so busy doing the rowing that I often didn't even notice that my partner wasn't loving me as much as I loved him, or giving to me as much as I gave to him. When you work hard to be a good giver, you don't stop and ask yourself if you are receiving anything back.

Why Women Fill in the Blanks

There are three reasons why many women get into the habit of giving more than they get in love, by filling in the blanks.

1. You feel you have to earn love. If you feel you don't deserve to be loved unless you do something to earn it, you will work hard to fill in the blanks in your relationships with men. Perhaps you weren't loved enough as a child; perhaps you felt you have to prove yourself to one or both of your parents in order to get their approval. Perhaps, like me, you concluded as a little girl that if you were loving enough, the men you loved wouldn't leave you. Whatever the reason, the result is the same: you become an expert at working hard for love.

2. You feel the relationship will fall apart if you don't fill in the blanks. If you've been with men who were "emotionally lazy," or saw your mother filling in the blanks for your father, you may believe that unless you fill in the blanks, your relationship will end, or not be very satisfying. Or, you may be in a relationship where you are putting up with less than adequate emotional involvement and contribution from your partner. By filling in the blanks, you can help "make up the difference." Then you can look at the relationship, see how loving it appears to be, and convince yourself that you are getting enough love after all.

3. Women abhor a vacuum. Have you ever walked into a man's sparsely furnished apartment and felt the urge to decorate it for him? When a group of people are sitting around, and no one is talking because they don't know one another well, do you feel compelled to start a conversation? Do you have a difficult time leaving drawers or closets completely empty, and feel the need to put something in each empty space? When you see a table set with only plates and silverware, do you feel it looks bare without flowers or something as a centerpiece?

If you answered yes to any of these questions, you will understand this point: women abhor a vacuum. Women like to fill things up, to connect things together, to create something where there was nothing. I believe this comes from our creative urge to give birth—to children, intimacy, beauty, conversation, or a coordinated bathroom.

In relationships, women feel drawn to filling up the vacuum: to fill the silences with words; to fill the distance with affection; to fill the time with activities; to fill the separation with love. This is a wonderful quality, and our ability to do it so well is a gift. But when we overdo it, we end up rowing the boat by ourselves.

How to Stop Giving More Than You Get in Love

If you've been reading this chapter and wondering if it applies to your relationship, there's a simple method for discovering whether or not you are filling in the blanks too much in your relationship: *Stop rowing!*

That's right, just stop. Stop making plans, stop running over to your partner to give him a hug, stop initiating sex, stop starting all of the intimate conversations, stop everything and watch what happens. If you notice that you aren't having any sex, aren't going anywhere, aren't spending intimate time with your partner, aren't talking about important issues, and aren't getting much attention, you will know for sure that you've been filling in the blanks in the relationship and your partner isn't doing his part. Then it's time to take some action.

1. Make a list of all of the ways you fill in the blanks. As a recovering "blank-o-holic," I read my own list every day to remind myself of what *not* to do in my relationship. Believe me, it isn't easy. Sometimes I am so tempted to plan the next four weekends for myself and the man in my life, or to tell him I love him every five minutes, or to fill every silent moment with conversation. When I find myself about to do something on my list, I stop, close my eyes, and think about all of the lonely boat rides I've had in my life and how much less I received than I gave, and I force myself to do nothing. Having a list will help you become aware of this habit.

2. Give your partner the opportunity to fill in the blanks. This is the second step of the process I just described. It means waiting for your husband to move over to your side of the bed rather than automatically cuddling up on his side; putting up with a pause in conversation, and allowing your partner to bring up the next topic; not always initiating sex, and giving your man a chance to seduce you; leaving your weekend free of plans, and when your partner asks what you're doing, answering, "You think of something. Surprise me." Take it from me—you may have to use all of your self-control to follow through with this. I am so used to filling in the blanks that it takes a conscious effort on my part to *not* give continuously.

One of two things will happen when you stop filling in the blanks.

▼ Your partner will rise to the occasion and start rowing himself.

▼ Your partner's true noninvolvement and noninterest in the relationship will be revealed, and you'll notice your relationship quickly deteriorating.

There's definitely a risk involved in not filling in the blanks. You may find out you've been in the relationship by yourself. You may discover that your partner doesn't have much to offer you. You may even realize that you are enjoying being loving, but that you don't love your partner in particular. But the risk is worth taking.

3. Make sure your life is filled with other creatively satisfying activities so your relationship isn't your only outlet for that creative energy. The more autonomous you are as a woman, the less you will look to your relationship to fill you up. Follow your own dreams, take good care of yourself, and make sure you are giving to yourself as much as to your partner.

4. Talk to the man in your life about filling in the blanks. If you are a recovering alcoholic, you know that part of your recovery is to inform the person you're in a relationship with about your disease, and to ask for his support. The same holds true with filling in the blanks. Tell the man in your life that you are in the habit of giving too much. Describe your favorite ways to do this. Ask him for his help in catching you in the act. Then tell him what you need from him, and make some arrangements about sharing the emotional load in the relationship.

This is an important step in asking for the love you deserve. At first, your man may appear to be resistant. Remember: he may be frightened that he is going to be loved less, so be sure to explain this information to him carefully.

It would be helpful if he could read this chapter himself. Hopefully, he will be willing to work with you on making your relationship healthier and more balanced, and you'll be well on your way to giving and getting the love you want.

WHATEVER HAPPENED TO THE QUEEN OF HEARTS?

For years I'd worked hard to master all the other aspects of creating a successful, loving relationship, but filling in the blanks had been one of my biggest blind spots, an area I hadn't been willing to look at. When I realized how much of my life I'd spent giving more love than I received, I made a commitment to myself that I would never work that hard to be loved again.

I'm happy to say that I'm in a relationship now with a man who loves me as much as I love him. For the first time in my life, I'm being loved without working to earn it, or performing to be lovable. Natually, I still catch myself thinking I have to earn love, and fortunately my partner catches me too, and reminds me to stop rowing so hard.

One day, very early in our relationship, my partner and I were discussing love and intimacy, and I was rattling on about how much I've learned and how hard I was working on myself. He reached out, took both of my hands in his, and in a gentle voice said, "Barbara, you don't have to chase after love anymore." His words penetrated deep into my heart, and I began to cry—tears of sadness for all the times that the frightened little girl in me believed she had to work hard to be loved; and tears of joy for the gift I'd given myself when I made a decision to stop begging for love, and for the gift of finally attracting a man with such a wonderful capacity to love.

So I'll end this section on how women relate to men with this reminder: *You don't have to chase after love anymore!*

SECRETS

ABOUT

MEN

4 Solving the Three Biggest Mysteries About Men

We've come to the portion of our "instruction manual" that you've been waiting for—solutions to some of the biggest mysteries about men. We'll look at what I call "the Three Big Mysteries About Men." I know that after reading this chapter, you will feel less and less like you're going crazy when you deal with the men in your life.

In my work over the past ten years, I've found that there are three questions that, at one time or another, have plagued every woman who has ever had to deal with a man— questions that women would love an answer to:

1. Why do men hate to be wrong?
2. Why do men hate it when women get upset or emotional?
3. Why do men seem to care less about love and relationships than women?

93

Mystery 1
_____

Why Do Men Hate to Be Wrong?

You and the man you love are driving to a party in an unfamiliar area of town. According to the directions, you should have arrived a half hour ago. The fact is, you know your partner is lost. You know he has no idea where he is going. You know you are missing the party. You calmly turn toward him and suggest: "Honey, why don't we stop and ask for directions?" And to your amazement, your partner responds with anger and hostility, as if you'd said, "Honey, why don't you cut off your arms and legs?" You hear things like:

"I know where I'm going, so stop bugging me."
"Look—who's driving, you or me?"
"I know that street is here somewhere. If you'll just give me chance, I'll find it."
"Okay, forget it, we'll turn the car around and go home."
"What, are you saying you don't trust me?"

If you're lucky, you may accidentally find the house you're looking for and get to the party after all. Or you may drive around for hours because your partner refuses to ask for directions. Or—and I know this has happened to many of you—your partner may actually end up driving you home and calling the whole evening off rather than admitting that he is lost! And as you sit there in the car, staring at this wonderful man you love, who has suddenly turned into a stubborn, defensive monster, you think to yourself, _If I were lost, I wouldn't mind asking for directions. Why can't he just admit that he is wrong?"_

You and your boyfriend have plans to spend Saturday evening together. At six that evening he calls and says, "I thought it would be fun to eat somewhere different tonight, so I made a reservation at a great Indian restaurant down-town. How does that sound?"

You answer, "Gee, honey, it sounds wonderful, but I had Indian food for lunch yesterday with my boss. I think I'd rather eat something different."

There is a long, tense silence on the other end of the phone. "Oh," your man replies in an icy voice. "Well, I didn't know that. Look, since you're so particular, why don't you pick the restaurant?"

"I'm *not* being particular," you answer calmly, "I just don't want Indian food. Why are you getting so upset?"

"I'm not upset," he barks, raising his voice. "It's just that you're so hard to please sometimes."

"I am *not* hard to please! All I said was I didn't want to go to that restaurant. Gosh, you make it sound like I told you you're a terrible person for picking the wrong place. It's no big deal."

"Oh, it's no big deal. So that's why we are in a fight, right?" your partner says sarcastically.

And you think to yourself, *I can't believe he is acting like such a jerk. Why can't he just admit that his choice of restaurants didn't work, and suggest a new one?"*

Do these stories sound regrettably familiar? I know you already know this, but I'll say it again:

Men hate to be wrong.
They hate being told they are wrong.
They hate even to suspect that they might have been wrong.
And most of all, they hate it when a woman knows that they are wrong before they know it themselves.

Here's the tricky part: Men feel they are being "made wrong," or told they did something wrong, when you aren't telling them that at all.

▼

MEN OFTEN MISINTERPRET YOUR SUGGESTIONS, ADVICE, AND FEEDBACK AS ATTACK AND CRITICISM

▲

When a woman innocently offers her husband a suggestion for doing something differently, or gives him information she feels will be helpful, or asks for something she wants more of, he doesn't hear what she actually says. He hears: "You're bad. You're wrong. You made a mistake. You aren't good enough."

What Women Say and What Men Hear

We Say	He Hears:
"Honey, why don't you stop and ask for directions?"	*"You're stupid.* You're lost. I can't trust you at all."
"I'm not in the mood for Indian food."	*"You made a mistake.* You chose the wrong restaurant. You failed me."
"I want to spend more quality intimate time together."	*"You're bad.* You aren't fulfilling me. I'm not happy with you."
"Maybe if you talk to your boss and explain, he'll extend your deadline on the project."	*"You're a failure.* You can't get things done on time."
"Why don't you try doing it this way?"	*"You're doing it wrong.* You can't figure it out by yourself."
(In bed) "Honey, can you slow down a little bit? Just hold me for a minute."	*"You're a bad lover.* You don't know what you're doing."

Isn't it frustrating to make a comment to the man you love and have him react defensively with anger as if you've said something awful? This is what causes women to feel they have to tip-toe around the men they love, to "watch what they say."

WHY MEN FEEL THEY ALWAYS HAVE TO BE RIGHT

To understand this mystery about men, we need to go back to our earliest upbringing, when we were little girls and little boys. In Chapter 1 we learned that men are trained to feel that their role is to master the outer world of action and accomplishment, rather than the inner world of thought and feeling. Little boys are taught that their value is in what they do and the things they achieve. They hear things like:

> "Good boy, Tommy. You threw that ball really far!"
> "Son, while I'm away on the trip, I want you to be the man of the house and help your mother do all of the chores."
> "You raked all of those leaves up already! That's great. Here's fifty cents."

Even traditionally "male" games all had some "doing" in them. Building blocks; Tinkertoys; model cars and airplanes—all these involved some kind of activity, performance, or measurable product. So, based on this, little boys conclude that *in order to be good, I have to do it right.* They grow up, and base their sense of self-esteem on their accomplishments and aptitudes:

▼

MEN EQUATE THEIR SELF-ESTEEM WITH ACCOMPLISH-MENT

▲

So when a woman appears to challenge a man's ability to do anything perfectly, he reacts defensively. He interprets her feedback as if she is saying, *"You did it wrong. Therefore, you are a bad boy."* Usually, he doesn't even hear the details of her suggestions or comments. After initially determining that she doesn't think he is doing something perfectly, his emotional reflexes take over, and he switches into "defensive mode." She's waiting for a polite response: he's feeling attacked and made wrong. No wonder we have a hard time getting along!

How I Became a Parking Garage Prisoner

Whenever I talk about Mystery #1, I always think of this true story from my own life which perfectly illustrates the lengths a man will go to rather than admit he is wrong. Years ago, I was involved with a man who had a difficult time ever acknowledging that he made a mistake. One evening, we had tickets for a Broadway show that was playing in Los Angeles. I got all dressed up, and off we went. My partner parked the car in the huge underground parking structure, and we proceeded upstairs to the theater, where we enjoyed a wonderful presentation. When the show was over, I followed my partner into the elevator and down to the level on which he had parked the car.

We walked down past the rows and rows of cars as he looked for his. Five minutes passed. Ten minutes passed. Now, I was wearing very high heels that night, and my feet were beginning to kill me. And it was cold in the lot, and I had only a light sweater over my shoulders. At this point I asked, "Honey, did you lose the car?" My innocent question was greeted with a dirty look that said, *How dare you accuse me of being lost. I'm a man, a warrior, a great explorer. Don't you trust me?* What my partner actually said back was, "No, I didn't lose the car. Don't panic. It's here somewhere."

"I'm *not* panicking," I responded, "but we've been walking around for ten minutes and my feet are killing me. Maybe we got off on the wrong floor."

"No, this is the right floor," he insisted. "I can handle it. Besides, the exercise will be good for you." (I swear to you that he actually said that!)

We spent another ten minutes searching for the car, he walking briskly ahead, me limping behind. Finally, I'd had it.

"Look," I said, "It's stupid to just walk around in circles. Why don't you find one of those guards we saw with the little carts and ask him to drive you around to find the car?"

You would think I'd suggested that he throw himself off a cliff, from the strength of his response. "I don't need a stupid guard to help me. I'm not lost. And if you weren't nagging me so much, I would have found it ages ago. You know, you're so inflexible. Can't you just be here in the moment?"

"I am here in the moment," I replied. "And in this moment, I'm cold, my feet hurt like hell, and I want to go home. So find the goddamn car."

Well, after another fifteen minutes of useless searching, my partner very reluctantly agreed to ask a security guard for help. He climbed into the back of the little white cart like a convicted felon being carted off to jail, and sent me glaring looks of anger every few seconds. Needless to say, the guard drove us to several other floors before we spotted the car—my partner *had* forgotten what floor we were on. On the way home, I thought that maybe if I teased him about getting lost, it would lighten things up a little bit. Instead, he became even angrier.

"I can't believe what a prima donna you are," he ranted. "Where's your sense of adventure? A hearty woman wouldn't mind taking a walk after a show. So what if it took us a while to find the car?"

"Adventure?" I yelled. "You were lost! Why can't you even admit it? Don't turn it around on me. I'm sorry, but wandering around a parking lot in high heels and a cocktail dress for forty-five minutes is not my idea of a good time!"

And as I sat there rubbing my sore feet, I couldn't believe that this man had cared more about being right than about my comfort, and that even now he couldn't bring himself to say, "I'm sorry, I blew it."

▼

MEN OFTEN HAVE A DIFFICULT TIME SAYING "I'M SORRY," BECAUSE TO THEM SAYING IT IMPLIES THAT THEY DID SOMETHING WRONG AND ARE BAD

▲

This incident happened years ago. Of course now, knowing everything I do about men and the mistakes women make, I would handle the situation very differently. But I certainly have gotten a lot of mileage out of that story, sharing it with women's and men's groups—the women laugh knowingly; the men blush and look sheepish. Each time, I feel maybe, just maybe, being a parking garage prisoner was worth the lesson that emerged from that evening.

How Geneen Helped Her Husband Stop Being Defensive

Geneen, a 37-year-old flight attendant, was happily married to Alex, 42, an attorney. "Our marriage is wonderful except for one thing," she confessed. "I feel like I have to watch myself when I talk to Alex. Everything's fine until I try to make a suggestion or offer a different opinion—then he either gets cold on me or blows up at the littlest thing. And forget about actually giving him some criticism; I don't even take the risk. I don't understand why he always misinterprets what I'm trying to say."

Like many women, Geneen couldn't figure out this mystery about men. I sat down with her and Alex, and took them step by step through a series of make-believe conversations.

"Let's say you're planning your weekend," I said to Alex, "and you suggest to Geneen that you both take a drive into the country on Sunday. Now, Geneen, if you didn't particularly want to go for a drive, how would you respond to Alex?"

Geneen thought for a moment, and answered, "I'd say,

'You know what, honey? I've had such a busy week, I think I'd just like to hang around the house together.' "

"Okay," I continued. "So Alex, when Geneen responds like that, how are you feeling?"

"I feel tense," Alex said. "I feel myself getting angry, and I'm not sure why, and I feel like I don't want to continue the conversation."

"And what do you feel like Geneen is saying to you, even if you don't hear the actual words?"

"Well," Alex answered, "I guess I feel like she is saying that my suggestion was a bad idea, that I should have known she wouldn't be in the mood for a drive, and that I'm not very good at planning things for the two of us. I feel funny saying this, but I suppose I feel like, when I don't do it perfectly, she is going to think I'm stupid, or a failure."

Geneen was shocked to discover that her very self-assured, financially successful husband felt like a failure, a "bad boy," when he believed he'd made a mistake. Alex and Geneen agreed to work together in being honest about their feelings: Geneen promised to watch herself carefully to make sure she wasn't making Alex wrong; and Alex promised to check with Geneen when he felt she was saying he was a "bad boy," and to believe her if she assured him she didn't feel that way.

Three months later, they called to tell me how well they were doing. "Things are so different," Geneen exclaimed happily. "The old patterns still pop up between us, but we both catch ourselves, tell the truth about how we are feeling, and give each other the reassurance we need. I feel more relaxed around Alex than ever before, and even when he does get a little defensive, I understand *why* he's doing it, and take it much less personally."

WHY WOMEN DON'T MIND MAKING MISTAKES

Now, you may be reading this section and thinking to yourself, *What's the big deal about making mistakes? I make mistakes, but I don't mind suggestions or advice.* Again, the difference lies in how little girls and little boys are trained. Little girls are taught that as women, our job is to make things better in life—to make Daddy more comfortable; to make ourselves more beautiful; to make the house neater. So when a woman makes a mistake, she thinks, *Okay, how can I fix this? How can I make it better?* We may feel badly about it; we may feel upset that we received negative feedback; but we will usually work on improving ourselves as soon as possible.

This is one reason that many women become so involved with self-improvement activities, such as reading books like this, going to counseling, attending seminars. And of course, the reverse is true as well:

▼

A MAN OFTEN FEELS THAT TO READ A SELF-HELP BOOK OR GO TO COUNSELING IS THE SAME AS ADMITTING THAT HE ISN'T DOING SOMETHING RIGHT, AND THERE-FORE, IS BAD

▲

Have you ever suggested to a man you love that the two of you go to a counselor, or take a relationships seminar—and had him react with sarcasm or anger? Now you can understand that he doesn't hear you making a mere sugges-tion—he hears you saying there is something wrong with him and he needs to be fixed.

Of course, I'm not saying men aren't interested in per-sonal growth. I've found more and more men attending my Making Love Work seminars over the past seven years. Now as many men as women attend on a given weekend. But it's important to remember that it's still a lot harder for men to reach out for help or work on changing themselves, and that those who do deserve all the support you can give them.

"DON'T YOU TRUST ME?"

You and your partner are away on a weekend holiday. It's time for dinner, and your partner is reading the guidebook to find out about restaurants in the area. You reach out and say, "Honey, let me see the book." Your partner glares back at you and responds, **"Why, don't you trust me to do it right?"**

Your husband has been having a difficult time at the office, and you're concerned about how he's handling the stress. You call up his best friend and ask him to talk to your husband and give him some support. When your husband finds out you asked his friend to intervene, he becomes furious with you. **"Don't you trust me to handle it by myself?"** he asks.

Lately you've become aware that a female acquaintance of yours has been flirting with your boyfriend whenever your friends get together. One evening after a party, you bring the subject up to your boyfriend, warning him about this woman's motives and telling him about her reputation for breaking up relationships. Your boyfriend acts offended and angry: "I know this already!" he exclaims. "I don't need you to tell me about it. **Don't you trust me to protect myself?"**

How many times have you had a man you love misinterpret your advice or feedback as a sign that you don't trust him? If you're like most women, you scratch your head and think to yourself, *What does what I said to him have to do with trust?* Here's the secret:

▼

SINCE MEN FEEL THEY SHOULD ALWAYS KNOW WHAT TO DO, THEY INTERPRET YOUR FEEDBACK OR ADVICE AS AN INDICATION THAT YOU THINK THEY DON'T KNOW WHAT THEY ARE DOING, AND THEREFORE, THAT YOU DON'T TRUST THEM

▲

I'll never forget the first time I discovered this secret about men. I was in the middle of a huge argument with my partner at the time over what I considered to be a stupid incident. He was writing a report and asked me for my comments. I read the report, and made some notes I thought would be helpful. As he read the notes, I felt him becoming more and more distant and upset. Finally, I asked him what the problem was. He insisted nothing was wrong, and said I was expecting great accolades for my notes. I insisted that I didn't need to be praised for my feedback, but that I thought he was acting very weird! Our discussion deteriorated into his accusing me of being an overemotional, needy woman, and my accusing him of being a shut-down, unexpressive man. After hours spent going nowhere, the truth finally came out—he felt that when I gave him negative feedback, I was saying that I didn't trust him to do it right. Even though he had asked me for my comments, and even though he agreed with them, the fact that I'd acknowledged that he hadn't done it perfectly triggered him into feeling that I did not trust him.

I remember feeling relieved to discover the source of the problem, and yet bewildered at how this man could make the intellectual jump from my saying "Here's a suggestion" to imagining that I felt like saying, "I don't trust you." As we calmed down and discussed this, he helped me understand how important the issue of trust is for men, and how easy it is for them to feel mistrusted.

Solutions for Mystery #1

1. Avoid using language that makes a man feel wrong.
Now that you're aware of how sensitive men are to feeling wrong, be careful that you don't make things worse by the way you express yourself to them. For instance, if your husband is driving and you know you're lost:

Don't say: "This always happens! You are such a space case! You never know where we're going."

Do say: "Honey, I would feel so much better if we stopped for some directions. It makes me feel nervous when we drive around like this. I know you're doing a good job, but the street numbers are confusing."

Don't blame, don't condemn, don't name call, don't generalize, don't make value judgments on his character or abilities—simply tell him how you are feeling.

Don't say: "You are bad for doing this."

Do say: "I feel sad/scared/hurt/etc. when you do this."

And of course, be careful of saying anything that your man might interpret as your not trusting him. Make sure to let him know that you *do* trust him when you're giving feedback.

Important: I am *not* suggesting that as a woman, you tiptoe around men and either avoid giving them negative feedback or "sweeten" it so you don't hurt their feelings. I am suggesting you communicate with sensitivity. And of course, if a man is mistreating you, or hurting you, don't worry about how he is going to take your feedback—*stand up for yourself!*

---

2. Discuss this information with the man in your life.
Men *love* to feel understood. So sit down with your man and

read over this chapter. Ask him if he can relate to what I've said, and give him a chance to express his feelings about this issue. Let him know you don't want to make him wrong, and that you want to work together with him so that you can give him advice and feedback without his feeling you are criticizing him.

3. Give your man lots of acknowledgment and praise. I can't overemphasize how much acknowledgment and appreciation men need—much more than you would ever imagine. Your man might not ask you for it; he might deny that he needs it; he might even act like he doesn't enjoy it when you do it. Don't believe him!

▼

SINCE MEN GROW UP WITH A LIFETIME OF CONDITION-ING THAT TELLS THEM THEY SHOULD KNOW ALL THE ANSWERS AND DO THINGS RIGHT, THEY NEED LOTS OF SUPPORT AND PRAISE, NOT JUST FOR THEIR ACCOM-PLISHMENTS, BUT FOR SIMPLY BEING WHO THEY ARE

▲

One of the most common complaints I hear from men is "I don't feel my partner appreciates me enough." You may feel you do appreciate your man; however, it may not be for the things he needs appreciation for, the things you take for granted—the fact that he goes to work every day; that he is trying to learn more about how to express himself; that he got a good deal on your new car. Ask your partner if he is getting enough praise from you for the right things. And remember: Don't be fooled by a man's air of self-confidence into thinking he doesn't need your support and praise. Take it from me . . . he does!!

MYSTERY 2 —————————————————————

Why Do Men Hate It When Women Get Upset or Emotional?

Laura is feeling overwhelmed by the rebellious behavior of her teenage daughter, Alyssa. Alyssa has been hanging around with a very fast crowd, and every day her attitude gets worse. Both Laura and her husband Lee have talked with their daughter, and warned her that she'd better shape up or she'll be in big trouble, but for the past week Lee has been working overtime on a project at work, and the burden of disciplining Alyssa has fallen onto Laura's shoulders. Earlier this morning, Laura got into a screaming match with her daughter, and has had a pounding headache ever since.

At about seven o'clock in the evening Lee returns home from work to find his wife doing the dishes. "Hi, honey. How was your day?" he asks Laura, and to his surprise, she burst into tears. "It was awful," she sobs. "I just can't take it anymore, Lee. Alyssa has become a monster. I've tried everything this week, and she seems totally out of control. She doesn't listen to anything I say. I feel totally lost. Where did we go wrong?"

"Now, honey, sit down and get a hold of yourself. Crying won't solve anything," Lee says in a calm, reasonable voice. "Here, blow your nose, and let's discuss this problem. I'm sure we can come to some workable solution."

"But you don't know what it was like," Laura cries. "I've tried reason, and it hasn't worked. Nothing will work."

"Calm down, Laura," Lee answers. "Let's take this one step at a time. First of all, exactly what has Alyssa done this week that you aren't happy with?"

"You don't understand!" sobs Laura. "You weren't here

this week. You don't know what it's been like. How can you be so cold?"

"Cold? I'm not being cold, I'm just trying to be practical. Getting hysterical won't solve anything."

"I'm not hysterical, I'm crying—you know, expressing my feelings, something you have such a hard time doing. And anyway, I don't want you to be practical." Laura screams, "I just want you to comfort me." Laura runs out of the kitchen and collapses, sobbing, onto the couch. She feels abandoned, alone, and misunderstood.

Eleanor and Adam have just returned from having dinner at a restaurant, and as they walk into their apartment, Eleanor says, "Adam, I need to talk to you about something."

"Now?" Adam asks. "It's already so late, honey."

Eleanor's voice begins to quiver and she answers, "Yes, now."

"Okay," Adam replies impatiently, "What's wrong?"

"Well," Eleanor begins, "it's just that lately you seem so distant. I know you've been busy at work, but we haven't made love in a week, and, well, I miss you." As Eleanor finishes what she's saying, she looks up at Adam, hoping for some sign of comfort. Adam stares back at Eleanor, squirming uncomfortably in his chair, saying nothing.

"Well," Eleanor says, "how do you feel about what I said?"

"I heard you," Adam answers. "I'm sorry you feel that way."

"Is that all you have to say?" Eleanor says accusingly.

"Oh, I get it," Adam says, "you have in your mind a specific way that I'm supposed to respond, and if I don't do it right, then you're pissed off at me?"

"No!" Eleanor cries. "I just want to feel you here with me."

"I'm here," Adam replies coldly. "Do you see me getting up and leaving?"

"You might as well not be here," Eleanor says, now

sobbing. "You're just sitting there like some cold mechanical person, while I'm here needing you to love me."

"Look," Adam yells, "you're the one who ruined our evening by bringing up a problem late at night. You're so goddamn sensitive—you're always overreacting to something. If you weren't such an emotional basket case, we could have some peace around here! I don't want to listen to this crap anymore!"

Adam storms out of the room, leaving his wife to cry alone and wonder how she ended up with such an unemotional, heartless man.

Have you ever had a problem, felt like you needed your man to comfort or love you, and when you reached out for help, had him give you a lecture or advice instead?

Have you ever tried to share your feelings of sadness or fear with your partner, only to have him accuse you of being too emotional and needy?

I've witnessed this pattern between men and women like the couples described above, and asked myself: *Why do men hate it so much when women become emotional?* Many experts explain that a man is uncomfortable when he sees a woman becoming emotional because he's uncomfortable with his own vulnerable feelings. I agree that this common observation is part of the problem. However, I feel the real secret to solve this mystery about men lies a little deeper in the male character, in three "secret" feelings men walk around with that women aren't aware of.

THE FIRST REASON MEN HATE TO SEE WOMEN UPSET OR EMOTIONAL

▼

MEN ARE BROUGHT UP TO FEEL THEY ARE RESPONSIBLE FOR FIXING THINGS

▲

As we've seen throughout this book, men are conditioned from the time they are still little boys to feel as though they are the responsible ones.

> "Now, Timmy, you watch your sister and make sure she doesn't get hurt."
> "When you grow up, son, you're going to be the head of your own house."
> "Daddy needs help carrying the packages in from the car, son."

These little boys grow into men who carry around an unconscious belief that *if I'm a real man, I will be competent, and will take care of the woman in my life.*

Is He Really a Jerk, or Is He Your Knight in Shining Armor?

When you approach your man with a problem that is upsetting you, he doesn't always even hear the words you are saying. He "hears":

> "Help me!"
> "Rescue me!"
> "Fix it for me!"

As a woman, you want to be:

> Reassured
> Comforted
> Hugged
> Listened to
> Soothed
> Told everything is going to be all right

Instead, you get:

> Advice
> Questions

Lectures
Blame for being so upset

You want love; he gives you logic. You want to be "mothered"; he acts more like a father.

I remember one incident in my own life that typifies this mystery about men. I was having problems with some of my employees at my office, and was feeling frustrated about their attitudes toward their job performance. I came home at the end of the day, stomped into the house and ran into the man I was married to at that time. "I am so mad I could burst!" I exclaimed and began to unload my frustrations about the situation in my business. My husband listened for a few minutes, and as we stood by the stairs in the front hallway, he proceeded to spend twenty minutes presenting me with a step-by-step business plan that would help to resolve my problems, pointing out what I'd done wrong in the past that had contributed to the present situation. I became angrier and angrier, until I burst into tears.

"What's wrong?" he asked. "Don't you like these ideas?"

"I don't give a _____about your ideas," I replied. "I came in here upset and just needing some comfort, and you end up giving me a lecture."

"Well, I'm sorry I didn't do it perfectly, the way you think I should have," he retorted.

Who was right and who was wrong? Neither of us. He thought he was "helping" me by offering his advice. It didn't occur to him that I would have felt even better if he'd held me on his lap, listened to me, told me everything would be okay, and just loved me for a while.

And I thought that he was being insensitive and unresponsive to my needs, when the truth was, he was giving me what he considered to be the most valuable commodity at that moment: Solutions for my problem.

Here's what you need to remember:

▼

MEN ARE SOLUTION ORIENTED

▲

When your man sees you upset about a problem, his mind instantly goes into automatic pilot and thinks: *Solution . . . solution.* He may not even have a solution, but that's not the point. He'll stall for time by asking you questions about the problem, or looking quiet and pensive. You think he's being an unresponsive jerk. He thinks he's being your knight in shining armor, coming to your rescue.

This explains why a man often becomes angry when you discuss a problem or show your vulnerability. It's not that he's angry at you—he's angry because

a. He feels responsible for finding a solution.
b. He doesn't have a solution and feels stupid and like he failed you.

This was exactly what was happening in the case of my employee problem at work. My husband heard me come in the door and complain about my situation at the office, and he instantly felt like I was asking him to help me. He began spouting off advice and suggestions, and the more he counseled me and didn't comfort me, the angrier at him I got. The more he saw me becoming angry, instead of feeling better because of his terrific advice, the angrier at me he became.

It took us hours of intense conversation to unravel what had happened that day, but it was worth it—that incident taught me the answer to this mystery about men. Like most men, my husband couldn't believe that I would have been satisfied just being listened to or held. "You mean, all I had to do to get you to stop crying and carrying on was to hold you and tell you it would be okay?" he said afterward. "You didn't expect me to make it all better?"

"That's right!" I answered. "I just wanted to know you were there for me."

THE SECOND REASON MEN HATE TO SEE WOMEN
UPSET OR EMOTIONAL

Here's another thing that happens inside a man when he sees his woman becoming upset or emotional: He feels that somehow he has caused you pain, and that therefore he is bad. Even if you are upset over something that has nothing to do with him, your man will still feel responsible for your pain, and guilty if he cannot take the pain and hurt away.

WHEN MEN SEE WOMEN IN PAIN, THEY OFTEN BLAME THEMSELVES FOR BEING THE CAUSE OF THAT PAIN, AND IN TURN, BECOME ANGRY AT YOU FOR "MAKING THEM FEEL BADLY ABOUT THEMSELVES"

One man I interviewed recently put it this way: "When my wife comes to me and she's upset, I have a hard time dealing with her pain. If she's worried about something someone else did to her, I feel angry that anyone would hurt her, and angry that now I am feeling pain too. And if she's upset because of something I did, I feel angry at myself for causing her pain, and, in a funny way, angry at her for being so upset, since it points out what a jerk I can be."

Have you ever wondered why, when you're upset or in pain and turn to your man for help, he turns his anger on you? Part of the reason is that he's feeling angry at himself, either for not being able to rescue you, or for hurting you in the first place. As we'll see in the chapter on communication, men often choose to express their frustrations in anger, rather than other emotions, because it is safer for them. So when you're sitting there listening to your man be angry at you for being so emotional, he's probably feeling frightened, humiliated, helpless, hurt, guilty, or any one of a spectrum of emotions other than anger.

THE THIRD REASON MEN HATE TO SEE WOMEN UPSET OR EMOTIONAL

Have you ever tried to share your upset feelings with your man and had him try to rush you through it or get you to "calm down" and stop? You just want to cry for a little while—he acts like you're having a nervous breakdown.

▼

MEN OFTEN MISINTERPRET YOUR EMOTIONALISM FOR HYSTERIA, ASSUME YOU'RE IN WORSE SHAPE THAN YOU ARE, AND BECOME FRIGHTENED THAT ONCE YOU START, YOU WON'T STOP

▲

As we'll see throughout this book, for most men to show strong emotions, such as helplessness or fear, they'd have to be in really bad shape. So when your man sees you really upset about something, he projects his own emotional standards onto you and assumes you must be falling apart! Men don't understand how deeply women can feel about things in the moment without it totally overwhelming their sense of emotional balance.

Men also assume that once you start crying or complaining, you won't stop. This is why they say things like:

"Are you just going to go on and on?"
"I don't want to get into a big thing right now—we don't have time."
"Here we go, we'll probably be up all night."

You might just need five minutes of their focused, loving attention, and they respond as if you expect a twelve-hour emotional marathon.

▼

MEN DON'T UNDERSTAND THAT WOMEN HAVE MUCH MORE EMOTIONAL RESILIENCY THAN MEN

▲

That means that as women, one minute we can be crying, and the next moment we can be ready to make love. One minute we can be angry, the next minute we can be totally forgiving. Men have a more difficult time shifting from one emotional state to the next. They assume we can't either, and panic when they see us very upset.

THE SOLUTIONS FOR MYSTERY #2

1. When you are feeling upset, tell your man exactly what you want from him. This suggestion will save you hours of fighting, misunderstandings, and frustration. It simply means that when you are feeling upset or emotional, and need to talk with your partner, make sure to ask him for exactly what you'd like from him. For instance, maybe you've just had an argument with a coworker, and come home and need to unload your feelings about the incident. Tell your partner: "I am feeling so hurt and angry at Joan from my office. I need you to listen to me, and hold me and comfort me right now. I don't need any advice, honey, I just want to release these feelings and feel you loving me."

Now your partner knows how to give you what you need. He won't feel frustrated when he tries to help you, and you become angry at him; he won't feel like a failure when he attempts to solve your problem, and you complain that you wanted a hug. Instead, he will feel like a success because he gave you what you needed.

Here is another example: It's late at night, and you suddenly realize you've been feeling neglected by your partner all evening. You look over at him reading on the other side of the bed, and you know he is tired, and not in the mood for a long conversation. However, you also know you need to express your feelings.

You say, "Honey, something's bothering me, and I need to talk about it before we go to sleep. I know you're tired, so what I'd really like is to take five minutes and tell you how I'm feeling, and then to just have you hold me for a few minutes so I can feel connected to you. If you want to talk tonight, that would be great. Otherwise, please think about everything I say, and hopefully we can find some time tomorrow to talk some more."

Now your partner doesn't feel he's in for a ten-hour emotional marathon, and he knows how he can make you feel better, even if the whole issue doesn't get taken care of that evening.

▼

MEN FEEL COMFORTABLE WORKING WITHIN BOUNDA-RIES. SO, GIVING YOUR MAN A *TIME LIMIT* DURING WHICH YOU'LL EXPRESS YOURSELF MAKES HIM FEEL SAFE OPENING UP AND LISTENING TO YOU

▲

Of course, there are times when your partner may not be able to give you what you want. Maybe he is just as upset as you are. Maybe he is angry at you, and doesn't feel safe opening up and holding you quite yet. But the more you explain these principles to the man in your life, the more he will understand that you want to be loved, and not rescued.

2. Don't exaggerate when you are upset—your man will take you literally. Sally is complaining to her husband Harold about her frustrations with her catering business. In the middle of the conversation she says, "I just don't know what to do. I feel totally lost. I feel like I am going crazy. I should have never started this business in the first place. I feel like firing everybody tomorrow, selling it, and just going away by myself for a month."

As Harold listens to Sally, he becomes more and more alarmed. When Sally is finished talking, she feels better, and he feels terrible. He thinks to himself, *"Boy, Sally sounds awful. She is just falling apart. She obviously can't handle the pressure. What am I going to do? We need the second income from her business. Maybe she's having a nervous breakdown.*

Now Harold's reactions to Sally will be based on what he thinks she said, rather than what she really needs. He will begin to give her advice about not giving up the business, and talk to her as if she is a crazy person. Sally will become more and more frustrated, feeling misunderstood and unloved by Harold. Harold will become more and more frustrated, thinking he is trying to help Sally solve her problems, yet seeing her reject his solutions. Finally, he'll blow up, yelling, "Nothing I do ever satisfies you." And Sally will sit there crying, thinking to herself, "All I wanted was for him to hold me."

▼

MEN DON'T INTERPRET WORDS LIKE WOMEN DO— THEY TAKE WHAT YOU SAY LITERALLY

▲

When you say, "I can't take it anymore," your man believes that you can't take it anymore. When you say, "I feel like you don't love me," he really believes that you feel that way. This explains why so often, when a woman expresses her feelings to a man, he will conclude that she is much more upset than she actually is—he has taken everything she said literally.

Be accurate in communicating your feelings to a man. And, if you do need to just unload without worrying about how it sounds, let him know in advance that he shouldn't take what you say literally. The best format I've found for this kind of emotional unloading process is the "Love Letter"

118 ▼ SECRETS ABOUT MEN EVERY WOMAN SHOULD KNOW

I describe in my book *How to Make Love All the Time.* It's an excellent way for both you and your partner to release emotional tension and get in touch with all your feelings.

3. Let your man know you don't feel totally helpless, so he won't feel obliged to rescue you.

Remember: Men feel responsible to fix things. So unless you let a man know that, even though you are upset, you aren't feeling totally helpless, he will feel obliged to rescue you and will give you advice instead of comfort and love. Take the time you need to express your fears and worries and vulnerability. Then, when you are finished, say a sentence or two to reassure him that you aren't a total basket case. For instance, after Sally tells Harold about her catering business, she might say, "I know there's a part of me that realizes it's all going to work out. I just need to talk to my employees and change some procedures so that things work more smoothly. And the truth is, I could never sell this business— it's been my dream for so long. But sometimes I get so frustrated with it, I just feel like exploding."

Now Harold knows that Sally was simply expressing her frustrations and fears, that she isn't totally helpless, and that he can love her rather than panic and rescue her. You may not know the solution to your problem. You may be frightened of what you are facing. But your partner will feel safer acknowledging your vulnerable feelings when he trusts that you're going to participate in rescuing yourself as well, and that you're not placing the burden entirely on his shoulders.

Make sure that, in expressing your vulnerable feelings to the man you love, your hidden message isn't "rescue me, fix me."

Stuart complained to me about this pattern with his girlfriend, Wendy. She would come to Stuart with her problems, either about her own life, or about their relationship, and Stuart would try to comfort her. But each time the same thing happened—no matter what Stuart said, Wendy would remain inconsolable. "I can comfort and reassure her for hours," Stuart said bitterly, "and she starts to get off of it a little bit, and then, all of a sudden, she sinks back down into despair again. It makes me feel like nothing I say or do matters at all."

In talking with Wendy, I discovered the source of the problem: Wendy wanted to be rescued. She wanted Stuart to prove that he loved her by taking responsibility for fixing her life. Wendy's dad hadn't been around much when she was a child, and now, as an adult, she was still playing "little girl," hoping to get the caretaking she never had.

IMPORTANT: Some men who have had prior relationships with women who do want to be rescued may interpret your first signs of vulnerability as your falling apart. Let this man know you are *not* a victim and don't want to be rescued, but simply want to be loved.

MYSTERY 3 ——————————————————————

Why Do Men Seem to Care Less About Love and Relationships Than Women Do?

"I know he loves me, but I always feel like the relationship is more important to me than it is to him."

"When I come home at the end of the day, I can't wait to see my husband. But when he comes home, he doesn't seem as excited to see me. I don't understand."

"I always do special little things for my boyfriend, like buying cards, or planning special evenings. If he loves me so much, why doesn't he think of doing these things for me?

Can you relate to these statements? Most women can, because most women have experienced that the men in their lives appear to care less about love and relationships than women do. The truth is, it's not that men don't care about love. But there are some secrets about men and relationships that we need to understand:

MEN DEFINE THEMSELVES PRIMARILY FROM THEIR WORK AND THEIR ACCOMPLISHMENTS; WOMEN DEFINE THEMSELVES PRIMARILY FROM THEIR RELATIONSHIPS

In Chapter 1, we discussed the historical background for the traditional male and female roles. We saw that to men, accomplishment meant everything—it guaranteed their physical survival. And women have always found their purpose in maintaining love relationships, between husband and wife, and between parents and children. So even if you and your partner both have full-time jobs, your perspective on the balance between love and work will be very different from your partner's. A 1978 study by Wagenvoord and Bailey found that 75 percent of the males interviewed said the most important part of their lives was their jobs, and seventy-five percent of the females interviewed said the most important aspect of their lives were their families.

As women, we tend to interpret this difference in priority as evidence that we love our man more than he loves us. This is not necessarily true! What is true is that:

IF A MAN DOES NOT FEEL GOOD ABOUT HIS WORK AND HIS ABILITY TO ACCOMPLISH, HE WILL HAVE A DIFFICULT TIME FOCUSING ATTENTION ON THE RELATIONSHIP

If the man in your life is feeling frustrated in his job, worried about a project, feeling pressured about money, or feeling stuck at one level of success with no room for growth, he will not be 100 percent emotionally available to you. A chunk of his attention, his mental energy, and his awareness will constantly be focused on his discomfort with work, whether consciously or unconsciously. It will be difficult for him to completely relax if he is not feeling like a success.

It's not that he doesn't care about you. It's not that he doesn't love you or need you. It's not even that he cares more about his work. It's that his work has a bigger influence on his sense of self-worth than his relationship with you does.

It's hard for women to understand and accept this reality. Our values are different from men's, in that no matter how successful we are in our careers, if our emotional lives aren't satisfying, we don't feel good about ourselves. To a woman, spending intimate time with her man is a reward, a relief, the treat at the end of the day, *not* a distraction or interference. And so we want our man to be able to drop all of his worries and concerns about work, collapse into our arms, and seek solace in the comfort of our love. After all, that's what we feel like doing when we come home. Doesn't it make sense that a man would feel like doing the same thing? The answer is: *No!*

Unfortunately, men's identification with their work as the primary source of nourishment for their self-esteem is also responsible for the fact that, until very recently, men have suffered more stress-related diseases than women— heart attacks; stroke; high blood pressure; drug and alcohol addiction. All these are caused or complicated by mental anxiety, overwork, and an inability to relax.

HOW MEN'S AND WOMEN'S BRAINS DIFFER

Here's the second reason men appear to care less about love and relationships than women do:

▼

A MAN'S BRAIN HAS A MORE DIFFICULT TIME SHIFTING FROM THINKING TO FEELING THAN A WOMAN'S BRAIN DOES

▲

I know you've probably suspected that men's brains are different from yours, and you're right! *The male brain is specialized*—that means, the right side of his brain deals with visual-spatial functions (like accomplishing physical tasks, hand-eye coordination), while the left side of his brain controls verbal and cognitive skills (expressing feelings, understanding abstract problems). Researchers have found that the right side of the brain develops more in little boys than the left side. The result is that little boys are less verbal than little girls, and most adult men are also less comfortable in this area than woman.

The female brain, on the other hand, is more generalized. That means both sides of the brain work together on problems. Here's how Dr. Jane Barr Stump describes it in her book *What's the Difference:*

> Some people feel this is why women are able to make faster decisions than men and are more perceptive. In addition, if one side of a woman's brain is damaged by stroke, the other side, which duplicates the abilities of the damaged side, can take over. . . . This is not true in men. If a man has a stroke, and the left side of his brain is damaged, he may lose his ability to speak because the right side of his brain handles only spatial problems.

WHY MEN GET STUCK IN THEIR HEADS

What does all of this mean for us and our relationships? I believe it explains why a man has a more difficult time shifting from "being in his head" to "being in his heart," from traditionally right-brain activities to left-brain activities. It's actually taking his brain longer to shift gears than it takes you or me. So when you and your partner are discussing financial problems, or having an intellectual conversation, and suddenly you want to be affectionate, to cuddle or get "mushy" together, you'll probably find your partner not "in the mood." He can't shift modes as quickly as you can.

Do you ever wonder why it takes your partner longer to unwind at the end of a day than it takes you? If your man has been focusing on right-brain activities for eight hours at work, he won't be able to walk in the door and instantly shift into a vulnerable, emotionally expressive person as easily as you are able to.

Have you ever noticed that when you and your partner go away together on a vacation, he tends to be more attentive, loving, and sexual with you? The same explanation applies: When you take a man away from his work, you not only remove the pressures and stresses of the workplace— you also give his brain a rest from the eight-hour-a-day habit of functioning in a right-brain, analytical fashion. This makes it a lot easier for your man to be emotionally relaxed, receptive, and available to you. He doesn't have to shift from one style of functioning to another. I've interviewed hundreds of women who have complained that their husbands are different people when they are away from work, and that they dread coming home from a trip, knowing that they are going to lose some of that emotional availability as soon as he sets foot in his workplace.

THE SOLUTIONS FOR MYSTERY #3

1. Share this information with the man in your life. Take time to discuss these concepts with the man you love, and ask him for his opinion on what you've read. Let him know how much you have learned from this chapter. Now, I am *not* saying that the next time your husband or boyfriend isn't being romantic or emotional, you should say to him, "Oh darling, it's perfectly all right that you are acting like an unemotional slug, because I know you're just stuck in your right brain at the moment!" But do show him that you understand.

Remember: Men love it when they feel you are understanding the way they behave rather than simply judging them for it. You may be surprised to find that, even though your man may be aware of *how* he appears less caring about the relationship than you do, he may not understand *why.* Thinking about the secrets we've revealed in this chapter might actually be a relief to a man who has perhaps doubted the depths of his feelings toward his partner, telling himself *If I really loved her, wouldn't I naturally be as involved in caring for the relationship as she is?*

2. Discuss ways you can help your partner find his sense of self-worth not just in his work, but in your relationship. I believe that for men to begin living healthier lives, they need to redefine their priorities away from a singular emphasis on financial accomplishment and toward more emotional accomplishment. It's so important for a man to understand the intangible value of spending an evening helping his son with his homework, or taking a walk with his wife before dinner, or calling his partner in the middle of the day to say "I love you" and get some love and support. Talk about this with your partner. Ask him how you can help make it easier for him to enjoy your intimate time together.

3. Talk with your partner about ways he can make a smoother shift from working mode to loving mode. You can help your partner feel less stressed and more a part of the relationship by discussing ways he can make a smoother transition from the work environment to the love environment. Here are some suggestions:

▼ *Discuss ways your partner can unwind after work:* exercising; taking a walk; lying down and listening to quiet, soothing music; meditating; getting a shoulder or foot massage from you. Watching the news on television or reading the paper are *not* the best ways to relax, since they still involve a lot of thinking and comprehension.

▼ *Don't barrage your partner with emotional issues or problems as soon as he walks in the door* at the end of the day. Give his mind time to slow down before you expect him to be in a feeling mode.

▼ *Don't forget to use these suggestions for yourself as well.* Remember, however, that even though you may also work full time, either at home or at an office, it is still going to be easier for you to relax into an emotional way of relating than it will be for your partner.

4. Make agreements with your partner about how each of you will contribute to the growth and intimacy of your relationship. Many women make the mistake of secretly expecting their man to contribute time and effort to nurturing the relationship, only to become disappointed when he doesn't. Instead of just wishing your partner would become more involved in the relationship, ask him to share his feelings on the following topics:

▼ What is his picture of the kind of relationship he would like to have?

▼ What kind of time and effort is he willing to contribute to working on the relationship?

▼ What methods would he like to use to build a strong relationship—reading books together; counseling; seminars; weekly talks?

▼ How would he like to handle problems and difficulties in the relationship (talk about them immediately; wait until the kids are asleep; write down feelings on paper)?

Discussing these questions will not only reassure you that your man cares about your relationship as much as you do, and wants to make it work, but it will also help him get in touch with how good he feels talking about these things with you. Making some commitments about how he wants to operate within the relationship will give your man more of a sense of "ownership" in the relationship. Of course, you should share your answers to these questions as well. Hopefully, when you are done, you will feel like a team—two people fully committed to making your relationship work.

I hope you feel excited after reading this chapter—excited about the possibility of experiencing more love and less conflict with the men in your life. The suggestions I gave you work equally well with your partner, your coworkers, your father, your brother, or your son. Of course, there may be more mysteries about men you have in your own mind that you'd like solutions for. I recommend that you find your answers in the same way I did: Ask men! You'll be surprised at how much men love to explain themselves to you, and if you ask the right questions, you'll come away with knowledge of secrets about men that will make you much more confident as a woman.

I wrote this part of the book because my own understanding of these three mysteries has totally changed the way I relate to the men in my life. I am compassionate where I used to be critical; I am patient where I used to be judgmental. And the more I show men that I really understand how they feel, the more I find they are willing to work on transforming themselves into the loving, responsive people they truly want to be.

5 Secrets About Men and Sex

How much do you really know about men and sex? Take this quiz to find out. Ask yourself if you think the following statements are True or False.

A Sex Quiz for Women

1. Men love women who are mysterious in bed.
2. Men are turned off by women who show that they like sex too much.
3. When a woman laughs and acts playful in bed, it makes men feel judged and uncomfortable.
4. Women care much more about men's grooming and hygienic habits than men care about these same habits in women.
5. If you tell a man what you want in bed, he will feel like you are trying to take control, and will secretly resent it.
6. It doesn't really matter to a man whether or not you like him to perform oral sex on you, as long as you like to perform it on him.

7. When a man has an erection, it means he's turned on and ready to have sex.
8. The main reason that men talk less than women do during sex is that men are afraid to open up and be vulnerable.
9. Men secretly feel that a woman who frequently initiates sex is too aggressive and doesn't give her partner a chance to feel like a man.
10. The best time to talk with your partner about your sex life is in bed.

If you think that *even one* of these statements is true, you don't know everything you should about men and sex. If you answered that *most or all* of these statements were true, be thankful that you're about to read this chapter! The fact is, all of these statements are false, and you'll find out why as we talk about the secrets every woman should know about men and sex.

SECRET 1 _____

Men Often Express Themselves Sexually When They Can't Express Themselves Emotionally.

Has this ever happened to you? Your partner approaches you to make love, only he doesn't feel particularly loving—in fact, he seems uptight and tense. You attempt to talk to him, but he is definitely *not* interested in doing anything but having sex. You sense something is wrong, and you're right—it's not making love that he wants, or even sex; it's relief from the intensity of emotion that he's feeling.

Here's what's happening: Often a man will feel disturbing emotions building up inside him. Perhaps he's worried about a project he's working on. Perhaps he just had a conversation with one of his elderly parents and is feeling sad at having to face their physical and mental deterioration. Perhaps he's feeling guilty for the insensitive way he treated you earlier. As we've seen throughout the book, most men aren't brought up to feel that it is okay to express vulnerable feelings like fear, hurt, helplessness, confusion, disappointment, regret. So either your partner won't feel safe expressing these feelings verbally, or he won't know how to. And suddenly, he's in the mood for sex.

▼

MEN OFTEN USE THEIR SEXUAL ENERGY AS A "SAFE" OUTLET FOR THEIR REPRESSED EMOTIONAL ENERGY
▲

Now, this might not seem to make much sense to you as a woman, since most women function in the opposite way. We have a difficult time feeling sexual when we aren't feeling emotionally safe. But it's important to understand that men use sex almost like a language to communicate their unspoken emotions. At times, it's the only acceptable way some men allow themselves to feel anything at all.

This pattern in men may cause several problems:

1. Your partner experiences a physical release during the sexual act, but doesn't resolve the emotional tension he's feeling inside.
2. You feel offended by your partner's use of your body to dump his frustrations.

How Gary Used Sex to Express His Frustrations with His Job

Gary, a 46-year-old president of a construction firm, and his wife, Fran, came to me, complaining about sexual incompatibility. "Sometimes I feel like Gary is just using me for a sexual release," Fran confessed. "I can feel that he is upset about something, but he won't talk about it, and instead, starts coming on to me real strong and being very sexually aggressive. I don't even feel like he's enjoying it himself, and I know it doesn't satisfy either of us."

I asked Gary to think back on the last time he and Fran had experienced this kind of "release-sex." "I guess it was last Thursday night," he answered.

"Okay, Gary," I said. "I'd like you to close your eyes, and tell me about any events of that Thursday that were disturbing to you."

"Well," he began, "that morning I had a run-in with my operations manager. He's been sloppy with his reports lately, and I was dreading having to reprimand him one more time for the same damn mistakes. That started the day off pretty lousy. Then that afternoon, I found out that we'd been outbidded for a construction job by another firm, and that was a real disappointment. I'd worked for two months trying to get this contract. So all in all, it was a pretty terrible day."

"Good," I responded. "Now I'd like you to picture yourself standing in the bedroom with Fran, as she described, and beginning to come on to her sexually. Feel yourself just as you were that night. I'd like you to tell me how you were feeling at that moment."

Gary thought for a minute, and then answered, "Tired, angry, discouraged. I guess I was feeling kind of like a failure because I didn't get that contract. A part of me wanted to just drop out of work and never go back—you know, go live on an island and be irresponsible."

"Were you feeling particularly romantic, or even turned on?" I asked.

"Now that you mention it, I guess not," Gary admitted.

"And if it wasn't sex that you wanted, what did you need at that moment?"

"Well, I guess I just wanted to feel close to Fran, to feel like she still loved me, that she wasn't disappointed in me, that at least somebody was on my side."

"What if Fran had just lain down with you and held you and stroked you and told you how much she loved you, and listened to you describe these same feelings you just told me. How would that have felt?" I asked.

"It would have felt great," Gary answered softly. "Probably a lot better than it ended up feeling after we had sex."

▼

SOMETIMES MEN REACH OUT TO WOMEN FOR REASSUR-ANCE AND COMFORT THROUGH SEX, INSTEAD OF ASK-ING FOR IT VERBALLY

▲

As you can see, Gary didn't really want sex with his wife—he wanted to feel loved. But at the time, he wasn't in touch with that need and didn't know how to ask for what he wanted. When Fran heard Gary describe how he was really feeling on that Thursday night, she felt relieved. "Honey, I wish I had known how upset you were," she exclaimed as she went over to give Gary a hug. "I knew something was wrong, but thought maybe it was how you felt about me."

Gary and Fran agreed to work together on the suggestions listed below. One month later, they returned to discuss the results. "Things are so much better between us," Fran began. "Whenever Gary is feeling speedy and tense after work, we take time to just lie down together, and I let him dump all of his frustrations and concerns. There have been a few times when he's started to come on to me, and I could feel he wasn't all there. I reminded him of what we've learned, and he's stopped, and just held me, and tried to talk about how he is feeling. It wasn't always easy, but the amazing thing is that after he shares his feelings with me, he feels more relaxed. I feel him more there with me, and we suddenly get turned on, but from love, not just to get off sexually."

"I have to admit, we're actually having more sex than we were before," Gary told me with a grin. "Fran's right—it's not always easy for me to ask myself what I'm feeling when I go into my automatic sexual mode. But each time I do, I feel better talking about it, and Fran is much more responsive."

The Solution

1. Talk about this pattern with your partner. Of course, don't have this discussion in bed, or during an actual occurrence of the problem. Have him read this section of the book, and ask for his opinion.

▼

Don't say: "I knew you were doing something wrong when you wouldn't talk about your feelings and just wanted to have sex."

Do say: "I want to make our sex life even better—why don't we try the suggestions in the book, and see what happens?"

▲

2. Whenever you suspect that your partner's sexual advances are covering up his suppressed emotions, make it safe for him to share his feelings with you.
Let's say your partner is suddenly becoming very sexual, and you feel like he's just looking for a quick release, and is actually upset about something else.

▼

Don't say: "Don't touch me! I know you are upset about something, and until you tell me what's bothering you, you're not getting any sex."

Do say: "Honey, I'd love it if you'd lie here with me and just hold me for a little while. I want to feel you close to me."

_____▲_____

Then, express some of the feelings you imagine your partner might be feeling, as a way to invite him to express his own emotions.

> "Boy, it's sure been a hectic week for you at the office, hasn't it?"

> "I want you to know how proud I am of you for taking on that extra project, even though I know it's been so difficult."

> "It must have been tough talking to your mother today, and hearing about your father losing his hearing."

> "I know how worried you must be about the extra bills we have this month. It's scary to have all these new expenses."

With practice, you can learn to make it safe for your partner to feel his own emotions by showing him that:

▼ You understand how he feels.

▼ You aren't judging him as being a failure for feeling vulnerable emotions.

You'll find, as so many women I've worked with have found, that understanding this secret about men will help you to create a much more fulfilling sex life.

_____▼_____

WHEN YOU MAKE IT SAFE FOR A MAN TO RELEASE HIS EMOTIONAL TENSION THROUGH VERBAL EXPRESSION, YOU INCREASE THE INTIMACY BETWEEN YOU, AND THE SEX THAT FOLLOWS WILL BE MUCH MORE PASSIONATE

_____▲_____

secret **2**

Men Feel Emotionally Rejected When You Reject Their Sexual Advances.

Your partner comes up behind you and starts kissing your neck and caressing your body. You know he's trying to tell you that he's in the mood to make love, but you're definitely not. What should you do?

▼ React with irritation and hope your partner gets the idea.

▼ Act bored and turned off and hope your partner gives up.

▼ Say something like: "Come on, honey, stop that. I'm not in the mood right now."

▼ Reluctantly let him make love with you, while you lie there and mentally go over your schedule for the following day or decide which clothes you need to take to the dry cleaners.

The correct answer is "none of the above," and here's why: Sex is a very primal form of giving for men, a way for them to offer themselves and be received or accepted, physically and emotionally.

▼

WHEN YOUR PARTNER MAKES A SEXUAL OVERTURE TO YOU, HE IS DOING MORE THAN ASKING FOR SEX. HE IS SAYING, "PLEASE ACCEPT ME; PLEASE RECEIVE ME"

▲

Your partner may be totally unaware of this motivation—but just try turning him down flat and watch his reaction. He doesn't respond as if you said you aren't in the mood for sex at that moment; he responds as if you rejected him personally. The majority of men I interviewed complained that when their partner didn't respond to their sexual advances, they secretly felt crushed, humiliated. They don't hear you say "I'm tired," or "not now." They hear "I don't love you; I don't want you. You aren't desirable. You aren't good enough." Your partner may not know how to express his hurt about feeling sexually rejected, and if this happens frequently, he may retaliate by turning off to you sexually, or seeking sex elsewhere. This is why:

▼

MEN LOVE WOMEN WHO AREN'T AFRAID TO SHOW THAT THEY LOVE SEX

▲

Many women still feel timid about expressing their sexuality with their partner, showing him how much they desire him, or asking for sex from him before he asks for it. When you aren't afraid to show your desire to the man in your life, it makes him feel safer sharing his desire with you. Remember: Men hate rejection! Always being the sexual aggressor puts men in the position of being the one to be rejected. So your partner will feel very grateful to you if he knows you are willing to take the same risk of being sexually aggressive that he is.

THE SOLUTION

1. Don't totally reject your partner's sexual advances. Before you get outraged, I'm *not* saying you should always say yes when your man wants sex. I am suggesting that you learn to understand the particular vulnerability a man has in offering himself to you, and that you receive him in some way.

Do say: "Honey, I'm kind of tired right now, but I'd love to hold you close for a while. Why don't we lie down together, and see how we feel in a little bit?"

Do say: "I love you, and I'd love to make love to you later, but right now I'm so tense from work that I wouldn't be able to love you the way I want to. Let's just cuddle for a while, and plan some time after the kids go to bed."

In other words, remember that when your partner reaches out to you for sex, he is really reaching out for love. Don't just say no; give him what he is really asking for by holding him, or acknowledging him or telling him how much he means to you.

IF YOU AREN'T IN THE MOOD FOR SEX WITH YOUR PARTNER, SAY NO TO SEX, BUT YES TO LOVING HIM.

Your partner will feel better, and who knows—after sharing some love together, you might find you're in the mood for sex after all!

SECRET **3**

The Erection Illusion

I knew this title would grab your attention! Here's a secret many women don't know about men.

IF YOUR PARTNER HAS AN ERECTION, IT DOESN'T NEC-ESSARILY MEAN THAT HE WANTS TO HAVE SEX, OR EVEN THAT HE'S SEXUALLY TURNED ON

I call this myth "the Erection Illusion." Since women don't have penises, there are many things about that mysterious organ that we simply don't understand. We assume that when our man has an erection, he is turned on and ready for action. That may be the case some of the time, but it isn't the case all of the time. Here is some information to think about:

An erection is caused by an increase in the flow of blood into the penis. There are several nonsexual causes for an erection:

1. It is common for men to wake up in the morning with an erection. This doesn't necessarily mean a man is sexually aroused—his erection is a physiological response that occurs during sleep and upon waking. Sometimes a full bladder can create pressure in the lower part of a man's body, causing an erection.
2. Friction or pressure on the penis from tight-fitting clothing or sitting for a long time in a scrunched position can cause an erection. The penis contains thousands of tactile nerve endings which, when they sense friction, cause increase of blood flow into the penis.
3. Extreme states of tension or stress can cause an erection. When a man is upset or anxious about something, the blood vessels in his body tend to constrict, his blood pressure elevates, and he may get an erection.

How does the Erection Illusion cause problems in our relationships with men? We misinterpret the source of our partner's erection.

▼ **We assume our partner is sexually turned on to us, and therefore we feel pressured to do something about it.** This can cause resentment and misunderstanding between you and your partner. I remember an experience I had many years ago with a man I was involved with. He was taking off his jeans before getting into the shower, and I noticed that he had a three-quarter's erection. He came over to give me a hug, since I hadn't seen him all day, and I assumed that he was letting me know he was ready for sex. I wasn't in the mood, but went ahead and satisfied him. Afterward he said to me, "Well, that was a surprise."

"What do you mean, a surprise?" I replied. "I thought you were turned on."

"No, I wasn't turned on at all, but that changed when you started touching me."

"But you had an erection. I thought you expected me to make love to you," I said with astonishment.

My boyfriend laughed. "You're kidding, you really thought that? No, those are really tight jeans, and they'd been rubbing against me on the drive home. I didn't even notice it until you pointed it out."

▼ **We assume something else is turning on our partner, and become upset.** Your partner wakes up in the morning with an erection. You start to grill him—who was he dreaming about? Or your husband is talking to a mutual friend of yours as you sit around the swimming pool. When he walks back toward you, you notice he has a slight erection. Did he get turned on by your girlfriend? Is he fantasizing about her? Because of the Erection Illusion, you might mistakenly assume something or someone other than you has turned your partner on.

THE SOLUTION

1. When in doubt, ask your partner if he's turned on or not. Obviously, sometimes the erection you see is not an illusion at all, but a genuine indication that your partner is indeed turned on, hopefully by you and to you. If you're not sure, ask your partner. Let's say you wake up in the morning, and your husband hugs you and you feel his erection. You're not sure whether he's indicating that he wants to make love, or if it's just a case of Erection Illusion. You have two choices:

▼

Choice #1: **Ask him if he's turned on and in the mood for sex or not.**

Choice #2: **Forget about being sure of his mood, and go ahead and assume he is in the mood. Trust me—he won't mind if you're wrong! If he wasn't actually turned on when you start, he will be soon.**

▲

2. Talk with your partner about the Erection Illusion. Remember: the man in your life is a much more legitimate expert on his penis than I am. So ask him what he thinks about this secret. Maybe he'll agree, and you can have an interesting discussion! Maybe he'll disagree and tell you that if you ever see him with an erection, assume it isn't an illusion! But I promise you that you'll learn something in the process.

SECRET 4 ——————————————————————

Your Man Will Make Love to You More Often If You Have Sex with Him More Often.

"Sometimes when my husband is engaging in foreplay with me, I feel like he really isn't into it. He's doing all the right things, but it seems like it's an effort for him, rather than something that's coming from his love for me. It's as if he's doing it to get it over with, so we can get on to the 'good stuff.' "

"I wish Bill was more romantic in bed. I know he loves me, but he seems impatient when we make love. I like lovemaking to be long and drawn out, with lots of cuddling and talking, and he is more into just having sex."

There is a difference between having sex and making love. Having sex is the physical act of sharing pleasure with your partner. Making love is the emotional act of loving and adoring your partner.

You can have sex without making love. You can even make love without having sex. And of course, you can have sex and make love at the same time, which is a really wonderful combination.

In my interviews with hundreds of men and women, the results were clear: Women would like more lovemaking from the men in their lives, and men would like more sex from the women in their lives.

Women want more

▼ Cuddling

▼ Long kisses

▼ Slow foreplay

▼ Talking about feelings in bed

▼ Emotional sharing during lovemaking

▼ Romance

Men want more

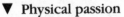

▼ Spontaneity

▼ Physical passion

▼ Playful, lusty sex

These different sexual tastes have their roots in the differences between men and women that we've seen throughout the book: Men are more focused on achievement of a goal; women are more focused on creating connection and intimacy. It's easier for most men to have sex than to make love, and it's easier for most women to make love than to have sex.

This doesn't mean women don't like just having sex, or men don't like making love. But these preferences are there.

Here's a secret about men and sex you need to know:

▼

MEN OFTEN SEEM LIKE THEY'RE MAKING A HALF HEARTED ATTEMPT AT MAKING LOVE TO YOU BECAUSE THEY SECRETLY JUST WANT TO HAVE SEX, BUT ARE AFRAID TO ASK YOU FOR IT

▲

Solving the Mystery of the Lazy Lover

This secret about men and sex was a great discovery for me, and I owe my understanding of it to my present partner. One night toward the beginning of our relationship, we were in bed and we began making love. After a while, I noticed that I was having a hard time getting aroused by what my partner was doing to me. This puzzled me, because normally we had an extremely passionate relationship. But for some reason his touches and caresses weren't having much of an effect, and I noticed he didn't appear to be as into it as he usually was.

I lay there feeling worse and worse, until finally I couldn't take it anymore. I sat up and said, "Listen, are you sure you're in the mood to make love tonight?"

"Yes," my partner replied. "I really want you."

"But you don't seem to really be enjoying loving my body like you usually do. Is there something wrong?"

My partner was silent for a moment, and then, with a sheepish grin on his face, said: "Well, to be totally honest, I'm feeling kind of tired and lazy, but I'm really turned on to you and I just want to fuck."

"Why didn't you just say so?" I asked in a surprised voice.

"It sounded so indulgent, and I thought you'd think I was being an insensitive jerk. I know how angry women feel about men who just want to have sex. So I decided to try and give you pleasure so I wouldn't feel so selfish. I guess you could kind of tell I wasn't really into it. I love you—it's just that tonight, I'm in the mood to have some good old-fashioned sex."

This conversation was a revelation to me. I thought of all the times I'd been with men who I knew were generally good, attentive lovers, but for some reason some nights seemed lazy, insensitive, and not totally present. I never suspected the truth—that they just wanted to be inside of me, to love me sexually, but felt too embarrassed and selfish to ask for it. After all, most conscious males of the 1990s are aware of the pre–sexual revolution stereotype: the self-absorbed man who spends two minutes pawing at a woman and two more pumping away at her and then wonders why she didn't come and wasn't satisfied. No self-respecting "liberated" man wants to appear to have any resemblance to that lusty animal. Instead, men force themselves to make love when they really are in the mood for sex. As women, we know something is wrong, but assume our man is just being a jerk, never suspecting that he's afraid to ask for what he really wants.

▼

THERE IS A CERTAIN KIND OF SPONTANEITY, SURRENDER, AND PASSION THAT MEN EXPERIENCE WHEN THEY ALLOW THEMSELVES JUST TO HAVE SEX WITH A WOMAN, WHICH IS OFTEN LOST IN A MORE CONSCIOUS, SLOW, STEP-BY-STEP LOVEMAKING PROCESS

▲

Men crave this lustful surrender as intensely as women crave the safety and tenderness of lovemaking. The mistake we make as women is judging our partner for wanting to have sex with us, and wrongly assuming that this means he doesn't feel as much for us as the other night when he did want to make more romantic love. The truth is that men would be better lovers when they do make love to us if we gave them permission to not always have to make love each time we have sex.

Important: "I'm *not* saying that in any way you should let a man be insensitive, abusive, or unloving when you have sex with him. I'm also *not* saying that if your partner is in the mood for sex, and you are not, you should grit your teeth and go through with it. Whether you are making love or having sex, you should always want to be doing what you're doing.

And this doesn't apply to you if your partner *never* wants to make love, and only likes to have sex:

IF YOU'RE WITH A MAN WHO NEVER WANTS TO MAKE LOVE, AND ALWAYS WANTS TO HAVE JUST SEX, I SUGGEST YOU EITHER HAVE A SERIOUS TALK WITH HIM, GET SOME COUNSELING, OR REEVALUATE THE RELATIONSHIP, BECAUSE YOU AREN'T BEING TREATED AS YOU DESERVE TO BE, AND YOU SHOULDN'T PUT UP WITH IT.

How Karen and Timothy Put the Passion Back into Their Marriage

Karen, a 36-year-old legal secretary, and her husband, Timothy, a 39-year-old computer consultant, came to me complaining about their sex life. "We seem to be out of sync with each other," Karen started. "Lots of times, I feel like Timothy is kind of rushing through foreplay to get to intercourse, and I end up getting very turned off."

"I try to please Karen," Timothy answered, "and I don't want to rush her. I'm not sure why she feels that way."

Listening to this couple, I suspected that they had not given themselves permission to have sex sometimes, without having to make long, romantic love. "Timothy," I asked, "can you think of a time when you were really turned on, and just felt yourself lusting after your wife?"

"Yes," Timothy replied. "Last week after we came back from a party."

"Tell me what happened."

"Well, we walked into the bedroom, and I was ready to jump on Karen right away. I went up and gave her a hug, and she hugged me back, and went into the bathroom to take a bath."

"Did you tell her you wanted to have sex?"

"Not in those words," Timothy said. "I didn't want her to feel pressured. I know how she likes it to be romantic. So I waited until she got in bed, and started to make love to her."

"I remember that night," Karen chimed in. "You seemed insensitive in bed for some reason, like you were mechanically doing stuff to turn me on."

"Were you feeling mechanical, Timothy?" I asked.

"Kind of," Timothy replied. "Now that I think about it, I guess I wasn't in the mood for a long, drawn-out process. I was feeling really horny and turned on to Karen, and just wanted to have some fun sex with her for a change. I suppose I felt guilty for feeling that way. Karen always expects me to be Mr. Romance and take my time seducing her, and I'm not always in the mood for that kind of lovemaking."

I asked Karen how she felt about just having sex with her husband sometimes.

"Well, I've never really thought about it," she answered. "I've always been really into making a ritual out of lovemaking. I guess just having sex seems kind of dirty, and I'm afraid that if Timothy did that with me, it would mean he didn't love me."

"Timothy," I said. "Tell Karen how you are feeling about her when you are in the mood for sex."

"That's easy." He grinned. "I feel like I just want to be swallowed up by her, like she's so gorgeous and warm and wonderful, and I can't wait to be inside her and feel her. I love you, Karen, and when I want to have lusty sex with you, it's *because* I love you, not because I don't respect you."

Like many women, Karen assumed that when her partner just was in the mood only for sex, he wasn't feeling as in love with her, or was just using her, or not caring about her. The opposite was really the truth—Timothy often felt so much love for Karen that it made him just burst with passion!

Timothy and Karen agreed to try an experiment: Timothy would tell Karen when he wasn't in the mood for long, seductive lovemaking, and Karen, if she felt like it, would try to enjoy having wonderful sex with her husband. Since Timothy had always been doing it Karen's way, she agreed that it was fair to try it his way once in a while.

The next time I saw Timothy and Karen, I immediately noticed a change in the way they related to one another. They were much more affectionate, and both of them appeared more relaxed. "I have to admit that I didn't like your suggestion that I try going with Timothy's mood for sex," Karen began. "But intellectually, I understood that I'd always been insisting he make love my way, and that I should at least try it. I can't believe how great it's worked out. One night last week, Timothy kind of grabbed me and told me he wanted me. I was really nervous, but threw myself into having sex with him. And when I stopped resisting the idea of what I was doing, I found I was getting really turned on as well. The truth is, Tim still paid attention to my body's needs—something I was afraid wouldn't happen if we didn't take a long time. And best of all, I felt totally loved the whole time. You were right—when Tim is lusting after me, he really is passionate because he loves me."

"It was great," Timothy added with a smile. "And the interesting thing I found was that a few nights later, I felt much better about really taking my time seducing Karen and not resentful because we were doing it her way. Now that I know she can have sex sometimes, I'm much less rebellious about making love the other times."

The Solution

1. Talk with your partner about having sex and making love. You may find, as hundreds of women I've advised have, that your man has been hesitant to express his purely sexual desires to you for fear of turning you off or offending you, or having you misinterpret his lust as being a sign that he doesn't love you. Ask him if he ever does a "rush job" seducing you because he really isn't in the mood. That may explain what you may have thought was his insensitivity or lack of expertise.

2. Give your partner permission to ask for sex once in a while. Examine your own judgments about sex. Since many women were brought up to think that girls who like sex are "bad," you may be suppressing your own purely lustful sexuality to avoid labeling yourself as a "bad girl." Women often try to "take the sex out of sex" in order to give themselves permission to have sex at all. Try having sex with your partner rather than always making a long production out of lovemaking. You may be surprised to find that, like Karen, you end up becoming very aroused by your partner's passion, and by the pure act of surrendering physically to your desire to unite with him. Be sure to talk about your feelings afterward. And of course, be sure your sex life isn't all sex the way your partner wants it, and never lovemaking, the way you want it.

3. If you're partner seems not to be totally there during foreplay, ask him if he's trying to get it over with because he's really in the mood for sex. Remember my story about feeling my partner was not really enjoying what he was doing to me like he usually did? Don't just lie there silently criticizing your partner for the way he's loving you. Ask him what's going on. Maybe he's in the mood for less seductive sex, and maybe you can try it. Maybe he's in that mood and you're not, and it would be better if you just held each other for a while that night. (Of course, this assumes that you know this person well and are confident that normally he really is a good lover.) For some wonderful techniques that will teach you and your partner how to make love and not just have sex, read my book *How to Make Love All the Time.*

SECRET **5**

Men Love Receiving Oral Sex From a Woman.

I know what you're thinking: *What's so secret about this?* Well, the secret lies not in knowing that men love oral sex, but in understanding why and looking at this sexual act from a different perspective. Almost 100 percent of the men I interviewed mentioned how much they loved a woman who loved giving them oral sex. The problem is that many women dislike performing oral sex for a variety of reasons— they think it's dirty; they think it's disgusting since men urinate from the penis; they feel nervous and unsure about what to do.

Here's a different way to look at oral sex: A man's penis is not only the most sensitive part of his body, but the most vulnerable. It represents his maleness, his sense of power, his identity. Men feel vulnerable having a penis in a very different way from the way women feel vulnerable having a vagina. A woman's vagina is hidden; a man's penis is visible. When a man becomes aroused, you can't miss it; when a woman becomes aroused, no one but her can notice it.

MEN DON'T LOVE ORAL SEX JUST BECAUSE IT FEELS SO GOOD—THEY LOVE IT BECAUSE IT MAKES THEM FEEL SO ACCEPTED, SO RECEIVED

One of the biggest mistakes women make when imagining giving oral sex to a man is thinking, *I'll be sticking this guy's dick in my mouth, and that's the same place he pees from.* Well, this doesn't sound very appealing, does it? The truth is, the essence of loving your partner orally has to do with loving and adoring his most vulnerable part. Sure, it feels fantastic to your partner. But more than that, it makes him feel received and accepted.

How I Taught My Best Friend to Love Giving Oral Sex

Let me tell you a story that I share with women in my seminars about a friend of mine I'll call Sue. This incident took place years ago. Sue was my best friend from college, and we were very close. I hadn't seen her for several months, and flew to the city where she lived for a visit. We sat in her apartment and caught up on each other's lives. "I'm so excited," Sue exclaimed, "I have a new boyfriend who I'm really in love with. His name is Andy. Our relationship is great, Barbara, but there's one problem."

"What's that?" I asked with curiosity.

"Well, I am embarrassed to admit this, but I hate giving him oral sex. I've never really gotten into doing that to a man. Andy keeps telling me how much he loves it, but it grosses me out, and I don't know what to do."

I thought about what Sue said for a few minutes, and then said, "Okay, when you put Andy's penis in your mouth, what are you thinking about?"

"I'm thinking, *I have Andy's cock in my mouth,* and then I feel sick."

"I thought so," I replied. "Sue, let me try something with you. Do you love Andy?"

"Oh yes," Sue responded, "I adore him. He's so sweet and tender and funny and kind, and I love being with him. I'd never want to do anything to hurt him."

"Okay, that's good. Now, Sue, I want you to hold out your hand, palm upward. That's right. I want you to imagine that instead of being a normal person, your Andy was only six inches tall. Imagine he's standing in your hand right now. If Andy was only that big, and you couldn't make love to him normally, how would you love him?"

"Well," Sue giggled, "I'd gently stroke him and kiss him and tell him how precious he was to me."

"Good," I said. "Sue, the truth is that your Andy does have a 'Little Andy.' And it is only six inches tall (or whatever!). It's his penis. It's the essence of the big Andy whom you love. And when you love that part of him, you're not just sticking his penis in your mouth—you're loving Little Andy. The next time you do that, try to imagine that this is the only way you can show your love to Andy, and express your feelings through what you're doing. Andy won't just feel like you're sucking on his dick—he'll feel you are loving and adoring him, the same way you'd want him to love and adore you during oral sex."

Sue loved this idea, and agreed to try it and tell me the outcome. I didn't have to wait long. The next morning she called me at my hotel. "Barbara, I have to tell you that I just spent the most wonderful night of my life in bed with Andy.

I did what you suggested, and it worked! I loved giving Andy oral sex, and he was surprised and overjoyed. I thank you, Andy thanks you, and Little Andy thanks you!"

This happened over ten years ago. Sue's now happily married to another man, and they have a daughter. We're still very close, even though we rarely see each other since we live in different parts of the country. But once in a while when we talk on the phone, we'll laugh about this story and repeat those words: *I thank you, Andy thanks you, and Little Andy thanks you.* I hope that wherever Little Andy is, he's very happy.

WHAT MEN HATE ABOUT HOW WOMEN PERFORM ORAL SEX

Here's a list of the most frequent complaints I've heard from men about how women perform oral sex:

1. Women who suck on a penis as if they're trying to milk a cow with their mouth. We have all heard the expression "suck a man's cock." Many women make the mistake of thinking that men actually want to be sucked on hard, and they lie there and suck away as if they're trying to milk a cow or, as one man put it, "like she's trying to suck the life out of me." Every man has different preferences, but most men enjoy being stroked, licked, and surrounded by your mouth, and not simply being sucked on.

2. Women whose teeth scrape a man's penis. *Ouch!* So many men complained to me about this. "Tell women to watch their teeth!" they pleaded. A man's penis is very sensitive. Most men do not enjoy being bitten, nicked, or chewed on. Practice keeping your lips away from your teeth, and your man will be a lot happier.

3. Women who only put their mouth on the penis and ignore the rest of the body. "I hate it when a woman puts her mouth on my penis but doesn't touch it with her hands, or caress my testicles or my chest or legs while she's doing it." Many men expressed this same desire—they want to be loved all over, not just to have you put your mouth on them for five minutes and ignore the rest of them while you're doing it. Not only does it turn them on more to feel sensations in other parts of the body, but it makes them feel less self-conscious and more accepted when you use your hands as well as your mouth.

4. Women who give oral sex in total silence. Ladies, I know you can sympathize with this point of view. Haven't you ever had a man give you oral sex in total silence, while you are lying up there wondering: *Does he like it? Do I taste okay?* Men feel uncomfortable when a woman engages in such an intimate act as giving oral sex and doesn't say a thing the whole time. Obviously, it's hard to talk with your mouth full. But you can stop for a second and tell your partner how good he feels, how much you love him, how beautiful and manly he is. He'll appreciate it.

5. Women who spit out men's semen. To swallow or not to swallow: that is the question. This is a delicate issue. I'll tell you this much: Many men are very offended when they come in your mouth and you race off to the bathroom and spit it into the sink, or rush over to the side of the bed frantically searching for a tissue, or worst of all, pull your mouth away when your partner starts to ejaculate and let him just shoot off into space. It makes men feel rejected in a very significant way, as if you're spitting out their essence and not wanting to receive them. It makes them feel embarrassed, as if you think they're disgusting. It makes men feel dirty, as if you forced yourself to give them oral sex.

In traditional Chinese and Indian sexual philosophies, a man's semen is thought of as a precious and potent elixir, containing a high concentration of the life force. The semen, therefore, is regarded as something never to be wasted, but to be used in a way that energizes. Receiving a man's semen into your body, either through your vagina or through your mouth, is an offering from him to you of his own life energy. Some Eastern philosophies, such as that of Tantra Yoga, even believe that a man's semen has regenerative and restorative properties, making it a unique "potion" that promotes health and long life.

I know what you are thinking: *But it doesn't always taste good!* Since semen is a body fluid produced by your partner, its taste and quality will reflect his physical health. Drugs, alcohol, stress, and diet all greatly affect the taste and consistency of a man's semen. I'm not aware of any formal scientific research on this subject, but I do know from my own experience and from working with couples that changing your diet can create a dramatic change in semen taste. If you don't believe me, you and your partner should try it yourselves.

For instance, try having your partner drink a lot of pineapple juice for several days, and then taste his semen—believe me, it will be very sweet! I've also found that when a man drinks a lot of bitter beverages, such as coffee or alcohol, his semen will tend to have a bitter taste to it. A man who eats a lot of animal proteins (especially red meat), which dump acid by-products into the blood, will also tend to have a more acid-tasting semen.

If you feel your partner's semen is especially bad tasting, you might consider talking with him about experimenting with a modification in diet. Not only will you enjoy oral sex more, but he'll be a lot healthier. And here's something to do as a last resort: If you can't stand his semen, and he thinks you are overreacting by not swallowing it, give him a taste of it, and see how he likes it!

THE SOLUTION

I'm not going to tell you what to do about oral sex. I certainly don't feel you should ever do something you find objectionable. I hope, however, that reading this information has made you think, and perhaps you'll look at oral sex differently. There may be times when you feel comfortable loving your partner in this way, and times when you don't. You may not feel good doing this with someone you've only gone out with for a few months, but may find it more acceptable with someone you are deeply in love with who has also made a commitment to you. I do suggest that you discuss this with your partner as a way to learn more about each other and create more sexual intimacy between you. And don't forget to share all of your views about your mate giving oral sex to you.

SECRET 6

Why Men Don't Like to Talk and Have Sex at the Same Time

Have you ever tried to get a man to talk to you while he's paying his bills, or reading the paper, or talking on the phone? "Stop talking to me!" he barks. "I can't concentrate on what I'm doing." Aren't you amazed at what a difficult time he has doing more than one thing at a time? After all, as a woman you know you can be talking on the phone, watching TV, and doing your nails at the same time, and it's no problem!

Here's another question for you: Have you ever tried to get a man to talk to you while you're having sex together? Have you ever wondered why he seems so resistant to expressing himself? The answer to both of these mysteries lies in the same secret about men:

▼

MEN HAVE A MORE DIFFICULT TIME EXPRESSING THEM-SELVES AND SIMULTANEOUSLY PERFORMING A TASK THAN WOMEN DO

▲

In Chapter 4, we talked about how the male brain is specialized—the right hemisphere deals with hand-eye coordination and visual-spatial functions, while the left hemisphere controls verbal skills. Research has found that a male brain has to make a shift from one functioning style to another when a man shifts his activity. For instance, when your partner is making love to you, touching you, feeling you, looking at you, he's using one side of his brain, and when he wants to talk with you and express his feelings, he's using the other side of his brain. This shift requires some effort for men, whereas in women, both sides of the brain work together. For women, talking and having sex at the same time—or balancing your checkbook or watching TV at the same time—seems quite natural.

This difference between the male and female brain explains one of the reasons men have a more difficult time verbally expressing themselves during sex. We know that expressing emotions is already hard enough for most men, due to their cultural conditioning. But ask a man to express his feelings and at the same time perform a complex task like having sex, and you may be faced with a problem.

It's not that men don't want to share how they're feeling in bed. It just isn't something that comes naturally to most of them. You're lying there saying, "Oh, darling, I love you so much, I need you, oh, that feels wonderful . . . oh, I love being this close to you," and the only response you get is a few grunts and groans and some heavy breathing! You start to feel like your partner doesn't love you, or that he isn't feeling as intimate as you are, when in most cases that's not what's happening at all. He's just having a wonderful time playing around in his right brain. In fact, although he may know that you are speaking to him, his brain may not tune in enough even to hear the actual words that you're saying.

WHY MEN GET IRRITATED WHEN WOMEN TALK DURING SEX

We've said that men often feel pressured to perform, to do something right.

▼
_____

WHEN YOU TALK DURING SEX, YOUR PARTNER FEELS OBLIGATED TO RESPOND, AND THIS DISTRACTS HIM FROM THE LOVEMAKING EXPERIENCE
_____
▲

I know this may seem unbelievable to you, but I've been told this by so many men. Lenny, a 29-year-old architect, put it this way: "When I'm making love to a woman, and I'm really turned on and lost in the experience, the last thing I think about is talking. I'm too absorbed in the passion. If I hear her talking to me a lot, I start to feel pressured to say something back so she won't feel bad, and I have to stop and think about what I want to say. That pulls me out of the experience, and into my head. I guess I'm too busy feeling the love and closeness to talk about it."

By sharing this information with you, I don't mean to give you the message that you shouldn't ask your partner to express himself during sex. Hearing your mate tell you how much he loves you will help make lovemaking a safer and more passionate experience for you. But if you have a silent bed partner, and have been taking his lack of expression personally, understanding this secret about men may support you in feeling better about your sex life.

THE SOLUTION

1. Discuss this information with your partner. Ask him how he feels about conversation in bed. You may be surprised to hear him echo Lenny's thoughts—that he feels pressured to say something to you when you talk to him, and that he *is* feeling loving, but it's difficult for him to talk about it. Tell him your needs for verbal intimacy, and try to understand his needs as well.

2. Talk as much as you want, but don't be disappointed if you don't get a response. If you enjoy expressing your passion verbally, don't suppress it just because your partner doesn't do the same. Do, however, let your mate know that he doesn't need to feel pressured to respond, that you aren't fishing for an answer. This will allow him to feel comfortable when he hears you verbalizing your feelings.

3. Try making love without talking at all. If you suspect that you're a Sexual Blabbermouth, follow the advice I give in Chapter 6 for making love in silence. It will be a new experience for you!

SECRET **7** _____

Why Men Often Seem to Withdraw After Sex.

_____

"After Jerry and I finish making love, he always seems to retreat inside of himself. I'm feeling like talking and getting even closer, and he just lies there with his eyes closed. I know he loves me, but I feel shut out."

"I've given my husband the nickname 'The Frog,' because after we have sex, he leaps out of bed. He says it's to go to the bathroom, or get a drink of water, but I know he's trying to put distance between us. He laughs about it, too, and knows it bothers me, but he says that lying there afterward makes him restless."

I'm sure you've had this experience at some time in

your life, if not all too frequently—you feel your partner withdraw after sex. If you've been making love with someone you hardly know, who doesn't love you, then there's one explanation for his behavior—he got the sex from you that he wanted and is ready to retreat. But if you experience this with your husband or boyfriend, there's another explanation:

▼

MEN APPEAR TO WITHDRAW AFTER SEX IN AN AT-TEMPT TO GET "BACK IN CONTROL OF THEMSELVES" AFTER HAVING LOST CONTROL DURING THEIR ORGASM

▲

We've seen how important it is for men to feel in control in order to feel powerful. In *The McGill Report on Male Intimacy,* Michael McGill talks about why men aren't more loving and open with women:

> "The reason men are not more loving is that they want to retain power over themselves and attain power over others. . . . Men make of themselves a mystery . . . it is now apparent that they promote this mystery in order to gain *mastery.* . . . This controlling behavior, which is the absence of intimacy, thus serves two purposes for a man; it gives him the power he associates with success in life, and it protects him from feedback that might reveal his inadequacies."

Dr. McGill goes on to explain how power and self-image are so important to a man that the idea of disclosing himself or losing control is threatening.

When a man experiences sexual desire, he becomes more and more out of control, until he loses control totally during orgasm. This loss of control goes against all male conditioning, and therefore, it is at once blissful and frightening to him from a psychological point of view. In this way, sexual surrender is a much more powerful experience for men than women, as it contrasts with his usual attempts to be in control.

Perhaps now you can understand why many men appear to withdraw after sex. Jim, a 41-year-old divorced dentist, described this tendency with great insight:

> Most of the time in my life, I have to be the authority figure, the one in charge and in control. It's rare that I let that guard down. Sex is one of the only times I allow myself to really let go. I'm a very passionate guy, and when I make love to a woman, I make a lot of noise and really get off, and orgasm is very powerful for me. But afterward, I almost feel embarrassed, like I was caught being too needy, too emotional. It's as if during sex I became more like a woman, more surrendered, and when it's over I need to pull myself together again and get back in control, back to myself, back to being a man."

The Solution

1. Ask your partner's opinion on this information. If you aren't always satisfied with your partner's behavior after sex, discuss this with him. He may not know why he feels like withdrawing either until you explain this concept to him. Some men I know told me they were relieved to understand this, and that they've wondered if their tendency to pull away meant they didn't love their wife.

2. Agree on some afterplay that will satisfy both of you. Ask your partner what he needs after sex, and tell him what you need. Then come to a compromise. Some couples find that the man needs at least a few minutes to "recover," and then he'll be happy to talk and be more attentive. Find a solution that works for both of you.

SECRET 8 ——————————————————————

Men Are Turned On By Visual Stimulation.

——————————————————————

——————————————▼——————————————

Question: A man decides to make a deposit in a sperm bank. The nurse gives him a cup and leaves him alone in a small room for a while so he can produce a "specimen." In the room the man finds some magazines displaying very erotic photographs, and a book of erotic literature. Which do you think he'll choose to turn himself on—the pictures or the book?

——————————————▲——————————————

If you answered "the pictures," you are correct. Not all, but most men would choose the erotic photographs in order to become aroused as quickly as possible. That's because:

——————————————▼——————————————

MOST MEN ARE MORE "RIGHT-BRAIN," OR VISUALLY ORIENTED, THAN WOMEN, WHO ARE MORE "LEFT-BRAIN," OR VERBALLY ORIENTED

——————————————▲——————————————

In other words, men get turned on by what they see. This is why young boys choose to look at pornographic magazines for sexual stimulation whereas young girls read romance novels. This is important for us to understand for several reasons.

1. How you look will dramatically affect how turned on your partner is by you. I know you hate to hear this, but it's true. Your partner's primary source of sexual arousal is going to be how you look to him. This explains why men, become obsessed with a woman's, body parts, her weight, her lingerie, etc. When I interviewed men for this book, I was amazed to hear how many claimed that some of their major sexual turn-offs were baggy flannel nightgowns, saggy cotton underwear, and too much make-up (see Chapter 6).

2. Men will look at other women not because they don't love you, but because they are visually stimulated. Have you ever gone out to a restaurant with your partner and found that your eyes are on him, and his eyes are on every other woman around? I don't mean that he leers at women, just innocently admires them. You feel that if he loved you, he wouldn't look. He feels you're being unreasonable and possessive.

This is also a touchy subject, but the more I work with men, the more I find myself being more understanding and less reactive about it. The fact is that men are more visually responsive than women, just as women are more verbally responsive.

Your husband says, "Honey, watch where you're going—didn't you see that car?" You say, "Honey, why do I have to repeat myself? Didn't you hear what I just said?" Neither one of you is right or wrong—you're just different. The problem is that when we see men look at women, we assume they are feeling an emotional pull in that direction, instead of realizing it's simply a visual pull.

▼

Important: I am *not* saying that it is okay for a man in a committed relationship to flirt with or come on to other women. This kind of disrespectful behavior is very destructive to relationships. Even blatant ogling and staring is rude when you're sitting there next to him. But noticing beautiful faces and bodies, and admiring them are natural for most men, as long as they're also noticing and admiring yours as well.
▲

THE SOLUTION

1. If you want to turn your man on, make yourself visually appealing. Let's face it, ladies. Men will always be stimulated visually. You can rebel against that reality by deliberately neglecting your appearance so your mate can "prove" he loves you even when you look terrible, or you can accept the fact that your partner will be more turned on by you when he likes how you look. Consider dressing for his tastes and not just yours once in a while. Take him shopping and have him choose some outfits he would like to see you in, or some lingerie he finds sexy. You don't have to become a dress-up doll; nor do you have. to appeal to his visual fantasies each time you make love by showing up in a bright red garter belt and push-up bra. But if this is an area you've neglected, you may want to experiment with your choice of garments and check out the results.

2. If you are in the habit of making love with the lights out, try keeping them on, or illuminating the room with candles. Remember: Men get turned on in bed by what they see. While you're waiting for your partner to tell you he loves you, his eyes are roaming all over your body for a visual contact high. Give him some light so he can see you!

3. Talk about your partner's experience of looking at other women. Unless your partner is being an insensitive jerk and really makes a habit of blatantly lusting after other women, or unless your marriage is in big trouble, your mate is probably like most men in that he enjoys looking, but has no intention or desire to do anything more. Discuss this with him. Ask him how he feels when he looks at other women. If you want to be really bold, look at other women with him. If you see him admiring some woman's body, admire it yourself. "She does have great legs, doesn't she?" you can say. He might be shocked at first, or even a little embarrassed that you caught him in the act, but he will end up feeling close with you, appreciative that you gave him the space to look, and most important, he won't feel you are making him wrong.

I have an agreement with my partner that really works for both of us. I've told him I understand why, as a man, he enjoys looking at other women, and that although I am not thrilled by it, I can accept it as long as he looks at me in that way too. That means, if some woman walks by with no bra and a T-shirt, and he notices her breasts, I'd like him to remind himself how much he loves my breasts when he's done, and if not out loud to me, at least silently to himself. It's as if he can walk down the street and think, *There's a beautiful woman. Aren't women lovely? And look, right next to me, I have a lovely woman who is all mine. What a lucky guy I am!*

I know that understanding these secrets about men and sex will help you create a much more fulfilling sex life with the man you love. But we're not done with sex just yet. So take a deep breath and get ready to read about men's Top Twenty Sexual Turn-offs.

6 Men's Top Twenty Sexual Turn-offs

Here they are—the Top Twenty Sexual Turn-offs men have always wanted women to know about. I compiled this list based on hundreds of interviews and discussion groups I've conducted with men over the past five years. The list isn't arranged in any particular order—it just includes twenty of the most common complaints I heard. Naturally, each man has his own "favorite" top twenty turn-offs. I'm sure if you show this list to the man in your life, he'll find some turn-offs he agrees with, some he disagrees with, and some that he feels strongly about that aren't on the list. But I think you'll find that the ones I've chosen deal with information and issues every woman needs to understand.

You'll notice that some of the turn-offs listed seem to have nothing to do with sex. These are things women do that end up turning men off to them, and for this reason, they're just as important as the sexual complaints.

TURN-OFF 1
_____

Women Who Act As if They Don't Like Sex
_____

"She makes me feel like something is wrong with me for loving sex, like I'm some kind of animal, or that I'm less evolved than she is because she's risen above the need."

"I hate it when my wife acts like she's doing me a favor when we make love. She never actually says this, but I can almost hear her thinking, 'Oh, all right, let's get this over with so you won't bother me again for a week or two.' "

"I had a girlfriend once who was afraid if she showed me how much she liked sex, she would be 'dirty,' or like a whore. So she'd always play hard to get in bed, pretending to kind of endure the sex act, which made me feel like some kind of pervert."

These are actual comments from men explaining Turn-off #1: Women who act like they don't like sex. This includes women who:

▼ make derogatory comments about sex

▼ act embarrassed when talking about sex

▼ are frequently resistant to making love

▼ are critical of their husband or boyfriend when he expresses his sexuality

▼ have a "let's-get-it-over-with attitude" or act like sex is something to "endure."

WHY THIS TURNS MEN OFF

As we saw earlier sex is one of the only ways many men express their vulnerability with women. When a woman acts as if she doesn't like sex, it makes the man feel wrong, bad, dirty, embarrassed, and judged to be more unrestrained than she is. And you know from reading Chapter 4 how much men hate to feel wrong! It also makes a man feel like he isn't good enough—if he were a "real man," he would be able to make her want him. Perhaps a woman really does like sex but simply doesn't feel comfortable showing it. Nevertheless, her partner will still feel he has to "protect himself" from her judgments by turning himself off to her.

▼
A MAN WON'T STAY OPEN AND VULNERABLE TO A WOMAN HE FEELS IS MAKING HIM OR HIS DESIRES "WRONG"
▲

WHY WOMEN DO THIS

There are several reasons why women act like they don't like sex.

1. Myth: Men don't respect women who like sex. Many of us were told while growing up, "don't show the boys you like it, or they won't respect you—you won't be one of the nice girls they will marry." So we learned to suppress our own sexuality in hopes of not looking too loose, sleazy, or knowledgeable about sex. This myth couldn't be farther from the truth. Most emotionally healthy men want a partner who enjoys sex, since this helps the man feel comfortable with his own sexuality. So if you're still trying to play the "good girl," give yourself permission to relax and be the sensual woman you truly are inside.

2. You may like sex, but you may not be turned on to your partner or enjoy the way he makes love to you. A couple came to me recently for marital counseling. The man complained that his wife didn't like sex. I asked him to leave the room so she and I could talk in private. I asked her, woman to woman, what the problem was. "It's true," she confided. "I do avoid making love with my husband, but it's not because I don't like sex. I love sex. I just don't like it with him!"

If you are behaving as if you don't enjoy sex, ask yourself: *Would I enjoy sex more if my partner made love to me differently?*

If the answer is yes, talk to your partner about your sex life and express your needs and desires. It may be helpful to have a few sessions with a qualified sex therapist or marriage counselor, who can help both you and your partner begin to communicate more about sex.

Another cause for diminished sexual desire is the build-up of emotional tension in the relationship. As I discuss in my book *How to Make Love All the Time,* suppressed anger, resentment, and mistrust will eventually kill the passion between you and your partner. Work on healing the emotional relationship, and your sexual relationship will blossom again.

3. You may not like sex. If you suspect that you have a deeper problem than those stated above and that you don't enjoy sex, I suggest you work with a sex therapist to try to discover why you are blocking your sexuality. This is often the case in women who were sexually abused as children. Get help so you can be free to experience all of the expressions of love.

THE SOLUTION

The solution is to show your man that sensual, sexual part of you. Give yourself permission to enjoy your sexuality in and out of bed. Tell him you want him, show him you want him, and watch your man get turned on!

TURN-OFF **2**

Women Who Never Initiate Sex

"I hate the fact that my wife rarely initiates sex, because it puts me in the position of having to be the aggressor and taking the risk that she will reject me."

"The truth is, I feel very controlled by my girlfriend because she almost never comes on to me—she waits until I come on to her. Sometimes I know she wants me, but she still won't make the first move, and it pisses me off."

Men are turned off by women who never initiate sex. It makes the man feel controlled, teased, manipulated, and that makes him angry.

WHY THIS TURNS MEN OFF

If you rarely initiate the sexual activity in your relationship, your man ends up feeling that he's the one who has to take all of the chances. After all, it's an emotional risk to approach someone you love and let them know you want to make love. Maybe they won't be in the mood; maybe they won't be turned on by you enough at that moment to get in the mood. When you don't initiate sex at least a good portion of the time, your partner feels responsible for your sex life. And remember: Men already walk around feeling responsible in their lives. If they think you aren't sharing the burden of taking sexual risks, a part of them feels betrayed and angry and turns off.

WHY WOMEN DO IT

Women don't initiate sex for many of the same reasons they act as if they don't like it—we think initiating sex makes us look like we like sex (it does!!); we may be avoiding sex with our partner, or sex in general; we may use withholding sex as a means of controlling our partner if we are feeling powerless in other areas of the relationship. But it just ends up making men feel angry and frustrated.

The Solution

Same as for Turn-off #1: Go after that man of yours and let him know you're in the mood for some loving! Sure, he may turn you down sometimes too. But he'll end up feeling that you want him as much as he wants you, and that turns a man on.

TURN-OFF **3**
Women Who Act Unfamiliar with a Man's Body

"I was with a woman once who touched my penis like it was some ancient artifact. She was so timid to just hold it or rub it, as if she'd never seen one before, and I know she had. I couldn't even go through with the lovemaking—it totally turned me off."

"One thing I hate is that women always complain about how men don't give them enough foreplay and just go for the breasts and the vagina. Well, women do the same thing— they think if they kiss you and grab your cock, you'll be satisfied. Sure, it feels good when they do that, but it's not satisfying, and makes me feel they aren't really into making love."

You know how much you hate it when a man grabs your breasts, rubs your vagina a few times, and expects you to be turned on? Well, you may be surprised to find out that men feel the same way—they get turned off when you limit your foreplay to being what one man called a "cockgrabber." And it really upsets men when you handle their penis like it's a loaded gun that could harm you.

WHY THIS TURNS MEN OFF

▼ It makes them feel like a sex object—a hard penis you want to use—instead of someone you love and care for.

▼ It gives them the impression that you don't like their body or that you aren't educated about what turns them on.

▼ When you touch their penis without sensitivity or confidence, it makes them feel that you don't like their penis (don't laugh!), and therefore, you don't like them. As we saw earlier, men feel very vulnerable because their sexual organ is so visible.

MEN IDENTIFY SO CLOSELY WITH THEIR PENIS THAT THEY INTERPRET HOW YOU TREAT IT AS HOW YOU FEEL ABOUT THEM

One man explained it to me this way: "When a woman touches my penis like she's handling a small, vicious animal that bites, I feel like she's offending me in the worst way. I just totally turn off to her."

It makes them feel you are in a hurry to get them turned on, going right for the penis, so that you can "get sex over with." Remember: Men are brought up to believe that women don't really like sex anyway. So when you give them any indication that you aren't fully enjoying it, they feel rejected and embarrassed, and consequently turn off.

Why Women Do This

1. Penis fear: I believe Freud was wrong—I've met more women with "penis fear" than "penis envy." We've been brought up to fear a man's sexual organ, to feel it can hurt us, to mistrust it. Many women have never really taken the time to get to know a penis (I'm not kidding!), to feel comfortable with it. In addition, sometimes we focus our unconscious feelings of anger and resentment on a man's sexual organ, especially if we don't feel safe with him or totally loved by him.

2. If you don't enjoy making love with your partner you may tend to do what men suspect—focus on getting him turned on as quickly as possible so you can satisfy him and get it over with.

3. Women are often embarrassed to ask a man how and where he likes to be touched. We don't want to show him that we don't know, and so we act like we do. One man expressed it this way:

> I've been with women who I knew had no idea what really feels good to a man. They'd touch my penis as if they'd taken lessons from some bad porno movie, and then they would wonder why I wasn't getting very turned on. Sometimes I feel like women think a man's penis is so sensitive and responsive that all they have to do is look at it and he'll get hard. That may be true for eighteen-year-olds, but I'm forty-three and I need a little more attention than that.

The Solution

1. Make friends with your partner's penis! At the risk of sounding like Dr. Ruth, I want to give you this advice about becoming a wonderful lover—get to know your man's penis. Ask him how he enjoys being stroked, kissed, and caressed, and also how he does *not* like to be touched. After all, *you* *don't have a penis, so how can you possibly know how to make love to one unless you ask!!* Your man will be thrilled that you care so much, and you'll feel confident knowing that you are turning him on.

2. Make love to your partner's whole body, just as you want him to do to yours. Remember, just because your partner has an erection doesn't necessarily mean your work is over and it's time for intercourse. Learn to love and appreciate all of your man's body. This will give you time to become more aroused, and make him feel like you love every part of him.

TURN-OFF **4**

A Woman Who Makes a Man Responsible for Her Orgasms

"I went out with this woman once who drove me nuts. I always felt like I was passing the 'orgasm test': Can I figure out how to make this woman come? She'd told me she didn't always have an easy time having an orgasm, so naturally I wanted to satisfy her. But she expected me to be psychic or something. She didn't tell me what she wanted me to do or what worked for her. I guess she felt if I solved the puzzle, I'd be the right man. I used to get so frustrated, as I'd be touching her or eating her, and she wouldn't give me any clues as to whether or not what I was doing was what she needed. Sometimes, I'd be stimulating her for a half hour or more nonstop—my hand would be numb, my jaw would be sore, and she still wouldn't help me out. I finally stopped seeing her—it was too much work."

"It really turns me off when my wife blames me for the fact that she didn't have an orgasm. I could understand it if I wasn't sensitive to her, but I am. Sometimes, even after a lot of foreplay and long intercourse, she still doesn't come, and she makes me feel like I failed her."

Men do want to participate in helping a woman have an orgasm, but they don't want to feel like if she doesn't come, it's their fault. Women who put this kind of pressure on men are definitely a turn-off.

Why This Turns Men Off

▼ It makes men feel that performance pressure that we've talked about—that if he doesn't make you come, he isn't good enough, he's a failure.

▼ When you don't ask a man for what you want, he feels "set up," like you are about to test him to see how good a lover he is. A man interprets this as manipulative, secretly feels resentful and turns off.

Why Women Do It

1. Telling a man how to turn us on still embarrasses many women—it reveals the fact that we're one of those "bad" girls who likes sex, and that we want to have an orgasm, the height of self-indulgence.

2. Guiding a man to stimulate us to orgasm means admitting that we aren't naturally sexual goddesses who can come at the drop of a hat.

▼

MANY WOMEN WOULD RATHER LIE THERE AND FEEL FRUSTRATED THAN REVEAL THE FACT THAT THEY HAVE A DIFFICULT TIME ACHIEVING ORGASM

▲

THE SOLUTION

Love yourself enough to ask a man for what you want and need. Remember: It's not his responsibility to figure out how to give you an orgasm. He can, however, become a *loving partner* in your pleasure process. Talk about this outside the bedroom. You can take turns sharing what each of you likes and doesn't like in bed. If you're good at bringing yourself to orgasm when you masturbate, but find it more difficult when he stimulates you, tell him your favorite techniques!

Don't worry—your man won't feel insulted that you are offering suggestions. On the contrary, it will probably turn him on! This "verbal intercourse" is just as important, if not more, than the physical intercourse you participate in together.

TURN-OFF **5** ————————————————————

Women Who Are Sexual Traffic Cops in Bed

"I met Angela at a sales conference my company sent me to out of town. We hit it off right away, and ended up in bed that night. I should have suspected something was wrong when she started giving me instructions about how to undress her. No, don't take that off yet, go slower. Now take off my jewelry—carefully—and put it on the dresser. Things went downhill from there. This woman was a control freak. She wouldn't stop telling me what to do, and exactly how to do it. Faster . . . now slower . . . that's right . . . now move a little to your left—not like that, like this. I felt like I was in bed with an instructor. What a turn-off!"

"My girlfriend was married before, and had had a pretty unfulfilling sex life. I guess her husband was insensitive and selfish in bed, and Lori never felt taken care of. The problem is that she is taking it out on me by telling me exactly what to do in bed. I feel as if I'm being tested all the time—when I do something she doesn't like, she almost gets angry, and corrects me, which totally turns me off. I feel like she doesn't trust me to be a good lover without her help."

I introduced the Sexual Traffic Cop as one of my ten sexual characters in *How to Make Love All the Time.* This is a woman who has to be in control of the lovemaking. She gives a lot of instructions, corrects her partner when he does something wrong, and basically sounds like a cop giving directions. The Sexual Traffic Cop has an idea of how sex is "supposed" to look, and tries to get her partner to fit into her perfect picture.

WHY THIS TURNS MEN OFF

▼ **Remember how important is it to men to feel trust? When you give men constant instructions in bed,** it makes them feel you don't trust them to figure anything out for themselves, and turns them off!

▼ **When you give that many directions, it makes a man feel controlled and manipulated,** as if you are trying to take charge of the lovemaking. You become someone he's in a power struggle with, not a woman he wants to love.

WHY WOMEN DO THIS

1. You don't trust men to figure it out for themselves. Perhaps you've had some unpleasant and unfulfilling sexual experiences in the past, where your partner had no idea how to please you. This can turn you into a Sexual Traffic Cop. You unconsciously decide that you'd rather spell out every detail of what turns you on than risk another frustrating evening.

2. You feel powerless in other areas of the relationship and unconsciously use sexual instructions to gain a temporary sense of control.

3. You're used to being in charge at work, and approach sex as a project you intend to make turn out right. I've interviewed hundreds of successful business women who were so accustomed to giving orders for a living that they carried this habit over into the bedroom without realizing it.

THE SOLUTION

Talk about your sexual likes and dislikes with your partner when you aren't in bed, and when it comes time to make love, trust him to take the information you gave him and be creative. Give your man a chance to get to know your body, and learn how to love it the way you want to be loved. If he's still totally insensitive to you, perhaps you need to examine your compatibility, and how tuned in you are to one another.

TURN-OFF **6**

The Sexual Corpse—Women Who Are Unresponsive in Bed

"You know what I hate? A woman who just lies there while you make love to her . . . no sounds, no response, nothing. It makes me feel like what I'm doing isn't having any effect on her at all, like she's daydreaming or sleeping, or waiting for it to be over. It turns me off when women are that passive during sex."

"I wish my wife wouldn't be so reserved in bed. I know she loves me, but when we have sex, she acts so damn unresponsive. I'll say, 'Do you like this, honey?' and she'll answer, 'It's fine.' But for all I know, she could be dead, because she just lies there not moving, while I stimulate her. It makes me feel like I'm raping her sometimes, and lately I'm not even interested in making love that much.

The Sexual Corpse is one of men's major turn-offs—a woman who is very unresponsive in bed. The men I interviewed were very passionate about this complaint. They can't stand women who don't appear to be enjoying sex, let alone don't appear to be awake!

WHY THIS TURNS MEN OFF

One of the secrets we've learned about men is how important it is for them to feel successful, as if they've made an impact.

▼

WHEN YOU DON'T RESPOND, EITHER PHYSICALLY OR VERBALLY TO YOUR MAN'S LOVEMAKING, HE FEELS LIKE A FAILURE

▲

Classical psychological studies show that people will become much more upset when no attention is paid to them than if negative attention is paid to them. Lying in bed hardly moving, making no sounds of pleasure and giving no words of approval, will drive any man crazy and turn him off.

WHY WOMEN DO THIS

1. Because of the "I don't want to seem like a whore" complex, some women unconsciously give themselves

permission to have sex as long as they don't appear to be enjoying it. Moaning, writhing, panting, gasping with pleasure—all of these would give her secret away—she's having a great time; it feels fantastic; she loves sex!

2. For some women, playing the Sexual Corpse in bed is a way to express their suppressed anger and resentment toward their partner. It's as if they are saying, "See . . . I'm not feeling anything. You can't even turn me on, you asshole. You have no power over me at all." In psychological jargon, this is a very "passive-aggressive" response; the woman appears to be passively doing nothing, but her lack of reaction is actually a very aggressive statement.

THE SOLUTION

Give yourself permission to express your sensuality while you're making love. Practice telling your partner:

▼ How pleasurable what he is doing to you feels

▼ What you'd like more of

▼ What you'd like to do to him

▼ How good he looks to you and why.

Showing your partner how much you're enjoying making love is another way to share yourself with him and create a union, rather than just be two people trying to turn each other on. Beware, however, of overdoing the talking and committing Turn-off #7.

TURN-OFF 7

The Sexual Blabbermouth: Women Who Talk Too Much in Bed

"I knew this woman once who wouldn't shut up in bed. From the minute we'd start making out, she'd be talking, giving me a detailed running dialogue of every single feeling and sensation she was having: 'Oh God, I love your hot tongue in my mouth . . . you taste delicious . . . ohhh baby, I love when you hold me this close. . . . Now my nipples are getting hard, ohh yes . . . kiss them, that's right . . . just like that . . . oh, I love that . . . oh, your thighs, they are so strong . . . and on and on. I felt like I was eavesdropping on my own sex life! I know she was trying to turn me on, but the more she talked, the more turned off I got. A few times, I ended up with a headache, and I couldn't wait to go to sleep so I could have some peace and quiet.

"Sometimes I feel like my wife kind of upstages me in bed. She's telling me how much she loves me, how much she needs me, how she can't live without me. This goes on like an endless tape, over and over. I love her, too, but I feel like I can't get a word in edgewise. And even when I do express myself, it always seems so insignificant compared to everything she said. I know she feels like I'm not emotional enough in bed, but she doesn't give me a chance!"

The other extreme of the Sexual Corpse is The Sexual Blabbermouth, a woman who talks so much during sex that it turns her man off.

WHY THIS TURNS MEN OFF

▼ **It distracts him from experiencing pleasure.** Remember our secret about why it's difficult for men to talk and make love at the same time, since it means using two different sides of the brain? The same applies to listening to a woman talk in bed. When a man hears you talk during sex, his mind starts working to understand what you are saying. The more you talk, the more his mind works, until he's thinking, and not feeling anymore. Even though what you're saying may be exciting to him, just the mere act of focusing on your words will eventually pull his attention away from his sensations and turn him off.

▼ **When you talk a lot in bed, your man will feel obligated to talk as well.**

WHEN YOU EXPRESS YOUR FEELINGS TO A MAN, HE FEELS OBLIGATED TO RESPOND

Men assume that when you say something to them, you expect a response. We'll examine this more carefully in Chapter 7. In the case of sex, the more you talk, the more pressured your man may feel to respond. When a man feels pressured, he feels controlled, he becomes angry inside, and turns off. It doesn't matter whether you actually expect him to talk back or not—he'll still feel provoked to react.

WHY WOMEN DO THIS

1. When women feel nervous or self-conscious, they release their tension by talking. If you are worried about how your lovemaking will turn out, or you aren't feeling appreciated enough by your partner, or have emotions lurking under the surface that you haven't faced, you may find yourself becoming a Sexual Blabbermouth. Your talking distracts you from the unpleasant feelings inside of you.

2. Most women tend to be more verbal than men, and more identified with the emotional than the physical. So during sex, when you are experiencing very intense levels of sensation in your body, you may not know how to just relax into the pleasure and be in your body. Talking a lot puts you back on familiar ground, even though it will turn your man off.

THE SOLUTION

If you suspect you might be a Sexual Blabbermouth, try this experiment: Make a point of listening to yourself the next time you make love with your partner. Notice how much you talk, what you say, and what you're feeling inside. If you find you're talking too much, practice concentrating on the sensations in your body, breathing more into the pleasure, and focusing your awareness on your sense of touch rather than what you want to say. Try feeling more of the sensations rather than describing them.

For a real challenge, try making love with your partner sometimes and saying nothing at all. You'll be surprised how difficult it is (take it from me!). Of course, if you are a Sexual Corpse, forget this advice and practice talking as much as you can!

TURN-OFF **8**

Women Who Don't Take Care of Themselves

"I can't stand women who stuff themselves with junk food and then complain about how much they weigh, or that their skin is breaking out."

"You know what turns me off? Women with bad vaginal

odor who expect me to go down on them and perform oral sex. Don't they know how awful they taste?"

I don't need a woman to look like a model, but I definitely get turned off by women who have that frumpy look—sacklike clothes, hair with no style—I end up feeling like they don't care enough about me to make an effort to look nice."

I hate to break the news to you ladies, but men get turned off by our bad personal appearance habits just as much as we get turned off by theirs. They may not tell us they are turning off; they may even deny it. But believe me, it's happening. The list of complaints I collected in my research was astonishing. They included:

▼ Unshaved underarms and legs

▼ Bad breath

▼ "Moustaches"

▼ Unstylish clothing

▼ Unhealthy diets

▼ Overprocessed hair (too bleached, too permed, etc.)

▼ Wearing muu-muus or tent dresses around the house

▼ Unpleasant vaginal odor

▼ Flab

▼ Bad skin, covered with tons of makeup

▼ Body odor

▼ Chipped and peeling fingernail polish

I must say that the most frequently repeated complaint was bad vaginal odor.

Why This Turns Men Off

As we previously discussed, men are more visually oriented than women. It's very easy for men to become visually turned on, and it's just as easy for them to become visually turned off. Even though as women we have many of these same complaints about men, we're better at quickly transcending our judgments by tapping into our emotions. Men tend to get trapped more by the physical.

Why Women Do This

There aren't any profound psychological reasons why some women don't take care of themselves. It could be one of any number things—laziness; denial; lack of awareness; too busy with the kids; lack of education about health. The main point is this: Men get just as turned off (and maybe even more) when we neglect our appearance as we do when they neglect theirs.

The Solution

1. Ask yourself this question: If you were a man, would you be attracted to you? You'll never be physically perfect, but you can make yourself aesthetically pleasing to taste, smell, and touch, since that's what sex is all about. Make a list of what you can do to feel sexier—new hairstyle; body lotion on dry skin, and so on.

2. You are what you eat. If you eat junk food, you'll end up looking like junk. By the way, bad breath and body odor are usually signs of a poor diet. Make a commitment to a new, healthier way of eating. You'll look better, feel better, smell better, and taste better!

3. Exercise makes you look and feel sexier. Studies have shown that women who exercise regularly feel more sexual and enjoy sex more than women who do not exercise. You may have never thought of exercise as an aphrodisiac, but it is! Incorporate some kind of physical activity into your life, whether it's walking, going to a gym, cycling, or even dancing to your favorite music when you're alone.

4. Taste your own vaginal secretions. No, this is not a kinky new sexual act. It is a practical suggestion you may want to try in order to understand more about your body. I'm sure you're aware that the smell and taste of your vaginal secretions changes throughout your monthly cycle. If you are sexually active, I suggest dipping your finger into your vaginal fluid each day and checking its odor and taste. Now, if your reaction to this is "*Ugh!* That's gross!" then I have a question for you:

▼

WHY SHOULD YOU EXPECT A MAN TO PUT HIS MOUTH ON SOMETHING YOU THINK IS DISGUSTING?

▲

If you don't like the way you smell, or the way you taste, he probably won't either! Rather than be unpleasantly surprised and embarrassed when your man begins to give you oral sex and then suddenly changes his mind, know the condition of your body in advance. If you feel you don't smell or taste as fresh as you'd like to, you have two options: you can douche with a solution of water and vinegar (avoid those perfumed packaged douches—they're full of chemicals and irritants), or you can let your partner know you aren't in the mood for oral sex that evening.

Note: If vaginal odor is a chronic problem for you, check with your gynecologist. You may have an infection you don't know about.

TURN-OFF **9** _____

Women Who Don't Like Their Own Bodies and Put Themselves Down

"There's one thing my wife does that really turns me off—she's always complaining about how ugly she looks. We'll be dressed up and ready to go out for the evening, and I'll compliment her, and she'll respond by saying, 'No, I look terrible.' When I insist that she looks terrific, she'll start arguing with me: 'My hair is getting too long, and this dress isn't flattering to my figure—it makes me look fat' and on and on. By the time she's done, she's convinced me that she does look awful, and I'm totally turned off."

"I can't stand women who are ashamed of their bodies. You know, women who have to make love with the lights out so you can't see them, or who take off their clothes when you aren't looking and hide themselves under the covers. It's a real turn-off to me when I'm with someone who doesn't feel attractive."

Men take their cues from women. If you are constantly putting yourself down and pointing out what's wrong with you, he's going to start agreeing with you sooner or later!

WHY THIS TURNS MEN OFF

▼ **Men are turned on by confidence.** This goes back to all of their own conditioning that good equals confident and bad equals weak. So when you put yourself down, your lack of confidence is a turn-off. And the more you point out your physical flaws, the more he will notice them.

▼ **When you act ashamed of your body or overly modest, it makes a man feel that you think sex is** "**dirty.**" It puts him in the role of the aggressor, the bad person who is about to do something to you that you obviously are finding distasteful. *When you act like sex is dirty, it makes him feel dirty.*

WHY WOMEN DO THIS

1. We're trained to dislike our own bodies. As women, we're constantly being bombarded with images of the "perfect" physical woman—the tall, slender model in her early twenties without an ounce of fat on her body. Many of us judge ourselves to be not good enough because we don't fit the stereotype. So we become ashamed of our less-than-perfect bodies because they don't look the way we think they should. When you get around a man you love, you become even more self-conscious, frightened that if he really looks carefully at you, he'll discover that you're not perfect!

2. Women are trained to be modest and not show their sensuality. We're back to the "I don't want to look like a whore" complex again. Many of us still feel "dirty" when we admit that we love the way our bodies look and feel, or when we think about slowly undressing in front of a man. After all, "nice girls" don't do things like that, do they?

THE SOLUTION

1. Learn to love your body as the beautiful feminine expression that it is.

> Make a list of twenty things you like about yourself physically.
> Pose seductively in front of the mirror when you're alone, and see how sexy you look!
> Ask your partner what he loves about your body, and believe him.

And don't worry that he's going to discover you're not perfect—he already knows it, and he loves you anyway.

2. Stop putting yourself down in front of your partner.

Don't point out the cellulite on your things.
Don't contradict him when he gives you a compliment.
Don't complain about how you look.

If you don't like something about yourself, change it. Otherwise, don't talk about it. And when your partner tells you that you look beautiful, say, "Thank you!"

TURN-OFF **10**

Women Who Are Too Concerned with Their Appearance

"I can't stand women who feel that they always have to look perfect. You know, they spend hours on their hair and make-up every day, and the minute they get a little mussed up, they run to the restroom to fix themselves. I want a woman who can just throw on a sweatshirt and jeans and go out for breakfast without worrying about how she looks, who can roll around on the grass without being concerned about ruining her hairstyle."

"I went out with a woman once who cared so much about how she looked in bed that I got totally turned off. First of all, she came to bed perfectly made up, lipstick and all, and with loads of jewelry on—about four gold chains, bracelets, rings on half her fingers. She had these really long nails, the kind that look like claws, and she would touch me carefully so that she wouldn't break her nails. The whole time we were having sex, she kept arranging herself so that she looked good, stopping to run her fingers through her hair, or straighten her necklaces. I couldn't wait to get out of there!

Sexual Turn-off #9 was about women who neglect their appearance. Sexual Turn-off #10 is the opposite—women who are obsessed with how they look. The men I interviewed felt very strongly about this turn-off, and were quite specific about what bothered them.

1. Women who wear too much make-up. I heard this complaint hundreds of times. The fact is, most men hate make-up. They don't mind it when it's applied tastefully, especially eye make-up. But the big losers in my survey were foundation and blusher.

▼

MEN HATE IT WHEN THEY LOOK AT YOUR FACE AND SEE YOUR MAKE-UP, AND NOT YOUR SKIN

▲

Since we've been reading women's magazines all of our lives, we are used to a high-fashion look with make-up. But to most men, a lot of make-up looks cheap and makes us look uglier than before.

A special turn-off: Women who spend three minutes reapplying lipstick and lip gloss after dinner, right at the table while their man looks on.

2. Women who overdress. Although men appreciate women who dress well, they are turned off by women who always feel the need to be dressed perfectly, who have the appearance of spending hours coordinating an outfit, and who don't look comfortable in their own clothes. One man described taking a date to his son's little league game; she showed up in black leather pants, spike heels, an oversize white angora sweater, and loads of make-up. "She looked great," he explained. "That is, for a hot evening at a disco, but not to go to a baseball game with a bunch of nine-year-olds."

3. Women whose hair is untouchable. Men are turned off by a woman whose hairstyle says "Don't touch!" They dislike lots of hairspray, stiff styles, or hair they are afraid to put their hands into, for fear of being attacked by pins, combs, and other cosmetic weapons.

4. Women who are laden down with jewelry. "Why do women feel compelled to wear all of their jewelry at once?" one man asked me in jest. Men are turned off by women who wear too much jewelry and end up looking like Mr. T. We may think we look fashionable—they think it's gaudy.

WHY THIS TURNS MEN OFF

Have you ever had a man you love tell you that you look much prettier without make-up, and you think that he is crazy?

Many of the things we women do to ourselves to be and feel more beautiful seem very strange to men. They haven't been brought up surrounded by make-up, closets full of clothing, and drawers full of skin-care products (unless they had lots of sisters!) So although men appreciate women who take care of themselves, they are turned on by naturalness. **Men are turned off by women obsessed with their looks, because these women seem insecure and lacking in confidence.** Remember: Confidence turns men on. So if a man is with a woman who panics when he sees her without make-up, or who feels she needs to look perfect to be loved, he won't respect her as much as a woman who feels good enough about herself to show her natural beauty.

WHY WOMEN DO THIS

Unfortunately, women have been brainwashed by the advertising industry and the media to feel we must fit an image that these conglomerates have decided is beautiful. Of course, in order to become beautiful, we have to purchase products these same proponents of female image just happen to sell—make-up; clothing, and so on. Men are also affected by these images, and herein lies the double standard. Men say they want a woman who is natural, who doesn't take two hours to get ready to go out. And yet, if you do throw on your sweatshirt and jeans and go out with your man, no doubt he will be looking at the women who spent the two hours on themselves!

I love wearing make-up and getting dressed up, but I've also learned that there are times when it's more appropriate to be casual and natural.

▼

MEN APPRECIATE YOUR ABILITY TO ENHANCE YOUR NATURAL BEAUTY, BUT THEY ALSO NEED TO KNOW YOU CAN BE COMFORTABLE JUST AS YOU ARE

▲

The Solution

1. Ask the man in your life what his feelings are about make-up and clothing. This doesn't mean you should compromise your own tastes to suit a man. But many women have never really discussed this topic with the man they love. You'll both learn something in the process.

2. Practice being beautiful from the inside out. No matter how hard you work to look good on the outside, your real beauty always radiates from within. When you feel good about yourself, when you are taking good care of yourself, when you are maintaining your dignity as a woman, you will feel beautiful on the inside, and that beauty will show.

TURN·OFF **11** ⎯⎯⎯⎯⎯⎯⎯⎯⎯⎯⎯⎯⎯⎯⎯⎯⎯

Women Who Don't Like Receiving Oral Sex

"I was dating a woman once who I was really attracted to. We went out a few times and finally decided to sleep together. We were in bed, taking each other's clothes off and having a wonderful time loving each other. Things were heating up quite a bit, and I was kissing her thighs, and about to kiss her vagina when she cried, 'Don't do that!'

" 'But I want to,' I responded. 'I want to give you pleasure.'

" 'Yech! I think it's gross,' she answered.

"When I asked her why, she said she thought it was disgusting down there, and the idea of my putting my mouth there made her sick. At that point I felt myself totally turn off. I mean, if she felt her pussy was that disgusting, I sure as hell didn't want to stick my cock in it. I felt like saying 'Hey, baby, thanks for the warning!' "

"I love having sex with my wife, but I feel frustrated that she doesn't enjoy oral sex. She'll do it to me, but she won't let me do it to her. It makes me feel really selfish that I get to take but not to give; it feels like she's keeping a part of herself protected from me. Lately, I've been having sexual fantasies about other women, and no surprise, they all involve me giving them oral sex."

I was surprised to hear so many men voice this complaint during my research, and it brought to light one of the myths about men and sex:

⎯⎯⎯⎯⎯⎯⎯⎯⎯⎯⎯⎯⎯⎯⎯ ▼ ⎯⎯⎯⎯⎯⎯⎯⎯⎯⎯⎯⎯⎯⎯⎯

Myth: **Men are selfish in bed, thinking about their own pleasure and not about ours.**

Fact: **Men love giving pleasure to women—it's one of their biggest turn-ons.**

▲

WHY THIS TURNS MEN OFF

▼ **It makes them feel sexually selfish.** You know how much men love receiving oral sex. When you don't allow them to give this same kind of loving back to you, they feel selfish, dirty, as if the above myth is true. It's as if you're saying to them, "I'll do that disgusting thing to you, because you need it so much, but there's no way I'll let you do that to me. I'm better than that." The result is that they often end up being much more sexually aroused than you are.

▼ **It makes them feel rejected and excluded.** For many men, offering to give oral sex to a woman is a more intimate act than intercourse—they are connecting their body opening with yours. It is a way they can express their reverence and worship of your feminine essence, the most vulnerable part of your body. When you don't allow your partner to love you in this way, he feels rejected and excluded, as if there's that one last, most intimate part of you that you won't share with him. As one man put it, "She loves me enough to let me fuck her, but not enough to let me kiss her down there."

▼ **It makes them feel controlled.** When a man wants to give you his love in a particular way, and you won't let him, he feels controlled, as if you have the sexual power over him. There is always the hope that, if he does something right or pleases you, you'll give in and "reward him" with permission to perform the forbidden act. And when men feel controlled, they turn off.

Why Women Do This

1. We think cunnilingus is "dirty." Many of us were brought up and taught that "that place" between our legs was dirty. After all, we go to the bathroom down there, and menstruate, and it's the place that lures men to do nasty things to us that make us "bad girls." When we think of a man wanting to kiss us there, we become disgusted. Whey would he want to do that? When we focus on the location of that part of our body, we overlook the spirit of the act of oral sex—a man loving the most delicate part of a woman. Men who enjoy kissing your vagina aren't dirty—they are just being loving.

2. We are worried about how we smell or taste. Many women are too embarrassed to admit the real reason they don't like receiving oral sex: they're afraid they smell or taste bad. The solution to this is simple—give yourself a "taste test" as I described earlier in this chapter.

3. We've had a bad experience with oral sex before. If you've ever had an unpleasant experience with a man giving you oral sex, you may be very reticent to try it again: Men who slobber all over you; men who are rough; men who feel obligated to do it but obviously aren't enjoying it—these negative experiences can turn you off to ever wanting to be kissed down there again.

4. We feel that the physical experience is "too intense." If you have never enjoyed oral sex, it may be because you find the pleasurable sensations to be so intense that they make you uncomfortable. Your vagina has some of the most sensitive nerve endings in your body, and you may not be used to so much sensation. This intensity frightens some women because it is so powerful. One woman described it this way: "When a man goes down on me, it feels *too* good, like I'm out of control."

5. We feel that the experience is too intimate. Letting a man love you orally can be the most intimate sexual experience of all. For this reason, it makes you feel more emotionally vulnerable. This vulnerability frightens some women. They feel exposed, as if they have to protect themselves. Allowing a man to perform oral sex is a real act of surrender, and if letting go is scary to you, you may unconsciously choose to avoid that kind of sexual closeness.

THE SOLUTION

1. Talk about this information with the man in your life. Tell him your fears and your concerns; share any unpleasant experiences you've had in other relationships so he can understand your reluctance to try oral sex again. Just discussing your feelings will help break the ice and create more safety between you and your partner.

2. Ask your partner to tell you why he enjoys performing oral sex. Hearing your partner describe the feelings he has while giving you pleasure will help you understand more of his desire to do this, and you will think of it less as a mere sexual act and more as an expression of love.

3. If the physical experience is too intense, practice getting used to it in small doses. Some women report that experiencing small doses of oral sex helps them get used to that much pleasure, both physically and emotionally. Let your partner know you'd like to try this technique. Give yourself permission to lie there and relax, take deep breaths, and become one with the sensations, rather than thinking about what someone is doing to you. When it becomes too intense, ask your partner to stop for a moment and just caress you or hold you. Then, start again. This will help you build up your tolerance to so much pleasure!

4. Do a "taste test" if you're worried about offending your partner. Review our discussion of a "taste test," p. 183.

▼

Important: Don't ever submit to oral sex because a man pressures you to, or because you think you should. In spite of everything you've just read, if you don't feel comfortable doing it, don't! It's your body, and you should have control over what happens to it.

▲

TURN-OFF **12**

Women Who Are Sloppy Kissers

"I'll never forget this girl I went out with in college. She was gorgeous, and I had a huge crush on her. We went out once or twice before anything really happened between us. Then, on the night of our third date, we were sitting on the couch in her apartment and I knew the moment had arrived—I was going to get to kiss her. I was so excited I could hardly control myself. She leaned forward, and before I knew what was happening, she plunged her tongue down my throat and proceeded to kiss me like she was trying to clean my face. Now, I love French kissing, but this was ridiculous! I went from turned on to turned off in about two seconds!"

"I hate to admit this, but I can't stand the way my girlfriend kisses. She kind of opens her mouth as wide as possible, and moves her tongue around in the middle. I have a feeling she thinks this is sexy, and that it's supposed to turn me on, but it does the opposite. I like tender, soft kisses too. I may be a man, but I'm not some kind of animal."

When I interviewed men for my book research, I came upon this same comment over and over again—men resent being stereotyped as gross sexual beings who don't really care about the quality of sex as long as they're having it. Many men echoed the feelings of the boyfriend who wanted his girlfriend to kiss him more tenderly. And the consensus was clear: Sloppy kisses are gross!

WHY THIS TURNS MEN OFF

For the same reason it turns many women off—it has no subtlety; it has no sensitivity; and it can give you a chapped face!

WHY WOMEN DO THIS

We think it's sexy; we've never learned how to kiss well; we're nervous about our performance in bed and try to cover it up by plunging in, so to speak.

THE SOLUTION

If you suspect that you're a sloppy kisser, start by asking your partner how he feels about your kissing style. Don't just say, "Do you like the way I kiss?" Do say, "Do you ever wish I would try different ways of kissing you?" Then practice different styles of kissing. It will help to think of a kiss as a meal. Instead of always gobbling up your meal, try nibbling at your food sometimes, or taking smaller mouthfuls, or savoring each bite. You'll enjoy kissing more, and so will your partner—unless, of course, you are both sloppy kissers and like it. Then by all means, slobber away!

TURN-OFF **13**

Women Who Are Too Serious

"I've been involved with a woman for three years who I love very much. There's only one problem: she's too serious—about sex, about everything. I'm not a jokester, but I love laughing and fooling around, and when I do, she gets offended. Like in bed, sometimes I'll tease her, or talk in a funny voice, or something, and she says, 'Are you finished yet?' When she makes sex such a serious matter, I feel nervous, like I'm being graded or something. I wish she'd lighten up."

"Why is it that women think having a good laugh isn't ladylike? I love women with a sense of humor, especially when they can make me laugh at myself. I was in a relationship once with a woman who was great at this. One night we'd eaten a huge Italian meal, and came back to my place and started making love. Well, we were going at it for a while, but it was obvious that neither of us was even approaching orgasm. We were huffing and puffing, and working so hard. Finally she looked at me and said, 'Honey, I'm starving. I think I need another plate of pasta!' We both burst out laughing. If she'd gotten upset, or been really serious about our sexual mishap, I would have been embarrassed, and it would have ruined the whole evening."

A man's sense of humor is an important part of his psychological make-up. As we've seen, men are so hard on themselves, feeling pressured to always do it right, to be responsible, to be a success, that they need laughter to lighten themselves up. Joking and fooling around is a man's way to release emotional tension. Men become turned off to women who they can't share humor with.

WHY THIS TURNS MEN OFF

When a man is trying to be funny and a woman refuses to participate, **he feels like you are making him wrong, putting him down, acting as if you are better than him.** He may feel frightened that you are secretly judging and evaluating his actions and performance, especially in bed.

▼

WOMEN WHO ARE TOO SERIOUS REMIND MEN OF SCHOOLTEACHERS, MOTHERS, AND OTHER SCARY FE-MALE AUTHORITY FIGURES

▲

Men use humor to let the little boy inside them out to play. So when you don't participate, or show that same side of you, it frightens that vulnerable part of them, and their safety level with you diminishes.

WHY WOMEN DO THIS

Little girls are often taught that laughing and fooling around isn't "ladylike." We're also afraid that if we don't act serious, we won't be taken seriously.

THE SOLUTION

One man told me to tell women this: **Don't ever let a man feel that he's just made a tragic error in bed.** If he is touching you too hard, or too soft, if he accidentally pulls your hair, if he is lying on top of you and you can't breathe, don't react as if he just committed a crime. He'll feel completely humiliated, made wrong, and will turn off and shut down. See if you can find some humor in the situation instead.

Lighten up! Learn to laugh at yourself, both in and out of bed. Let your little girl out to play more. You'll have more fun, and your partner will be more turned on.

TURN-OFF **14**

Women Who Are Excessively Needy and Clingy

"There's nothing that turns me off more than a woman who is always an emotional basket case. You know, she can't make decisions for herself, she's paranoid if I even look at another woman, she won't let go of me when we go out together. Women like this make me feel trapped, suffocated, and no matter how beautiful they are, I lose my attraction to them real quick!"

"My big turn-off is women who are victims, the ones who always blame someone else for their problems, or seem on the verge of emotional collapse. I had a girlfriend once who threatened to kill herself every time we had a fight. I knew she wasn't serious, but she would become so helpless that it made me feel guilty for even disagreeing with her. After about six months, I had absolutely no sexual desire left for her at all."

"Weak, wimpy, whiny women turn me off." I heard this complaint from the majority of the men I interviewed. Men aren't talking about sensitivity or vulnerability, but about women who look too much to the man to fill them up rather than feeling self-sufficient from within themselves.

Why This Turns Men Off

The more needy and clingy you appear, the more a man feels responsible to rescue you. He becomes the parent, you become the child, and sexual desire disappears.

WHY WOMEN DO THIS

1. We feel powerless. In Chapter 2 we looked at the ways in which, as women, we act like little girls, give up our power, and put ourselves second behind a man. All of these self-destructive behavior patterns contribute to making us feel needy, clingy, and powerless. When you aren't centered in your own self-esteem, you will be much more insecure and needy in your relationship.

2. We feel afraid of loss. Whenever you lose someone you love, either as a child through your parents' divorce or death, or as an adult through a relationship breakup, you are much more susceptible to feelings of loss or abandonment. It's important to examine and release these emotions, as well as to understand how they can affect your love life.

▼

THE GREATER YOUR UNRESOLVED FEAR OF ABANDON-MENT, THE MORE YOU MAY TEND TO BE EXCESSIVELY NEEDY AND CLINGY WITH THE MEN IN YOUR LIFE

▲

---

3. We feel genuine fear because our partner is *not* loving us enough. Sometimes, the fear of losing someone you love is justified. Maybe he isn't treating you well. Maybe he isn't showing you how much he needs you, and you feel overly needy of him. Maybe he refuses to make a commitment to you. All of these male behaviors are legitimate reasons you might find yourself feeling needy and powerless in a relationship.

THE SOLUTION

1. Make sure you are owning your power and maintaining your dignity in your relationship. If you suspect that you are excessively needy and clingy with the men in your life, go back and re-read Chapters 2 and 3 to remind yourself how to live as a powerful woman.

2. Work on healing your fears of loss and abandonment. If you're aware that you have been carrying around unresolved fears of loss and rejection, make a commitment to emotionally heal yourself. Work with a caring therapist, join a women's support group, do whatever is necessary to unburden yourself of that old emotional baggage you've been lugging around from relationship to relationship.

3. Make sure you aren't filling in the emotional blanks in your relationship. As we saw in Chapter 3, you will inevitably feel unloved and needy if you are giving much more than you are getting from your partner. Take time to honestly evaluate your relationship.

TURN-OFF **15**

Stupid, Superficial Women

"I'll tell you what turns me off the most—women who have no idea what is going on in the world around them, and instead spend their time thinking about their nails, or the latest style, or watching television. I've met lots of women whose looks I was really attracted to, but the minute they opened their mouth, I lost interest. They just had their priorities all messed up."

"It's important to me as a man to be proud of the woman I'm with, to feel I can take her anywhere or introduce her to anyone and that she'll be able to hold her own. Sure, I like good looks and a nice body, but what turns me on the most is a woman with a great mind. That's my kind of stimulation."

Men in my survey agreed—women with superficial values turned them off. It's not that all men want a woman with a high IQ or an advanced education, or one who prides herself on being an intellectual. After all, men come in all degrees of intelligence too. But men do need to feel that their woman isn't simply a selfish, self-absorbed, superficial person. They complained about:

▼ women who read fashion magazines, but never *Newsweek* or *Time*

▼ women whose conversation consists of gossip about other women, TV shows they have seen, and information they picked up in trashy newspapers

▼ women who act dumb, frivolous, and bubbleheaded

▼ women who make no effort to continue to educate or improve themselves.

Now, I know what you're thinking: There are loads of men out there just like this who turn you off! That's true, but the kind of man you want to be with is going to want to be with a woman he feels is his equal, not his inferior.

WHY THIS TURNS MEN OFF

They might not admit it, but men often base their sense of self-worth on the kind of woman they have in their life. What other men think of his wife or girlfriend is important to a man.

MEN NEED TO FEEL PROUD OF THE WOMAN THEY LOVE

202 ▼ S<small>ECRETS</small> A<small>BOUT</small> M<small>EN</small> E<small>VERY</small> W<small>OMAN</small> S<small>HOULD</small> K<small>NOW</small>

In addition, since men usually feel more comfortable thinking than feeling, they need to know you can relate to them from your mind and not just your body. Men find a good, thoughtful conversation stimulating not just to their minds, but to their bodies as well.

WHY WOMEN DO THIS

As a woman, there's nothing that upsets me more than seeing another woman demean herself by acting stupid, using her body to catch men, ignoring her mind, playing the "bimbo," and not using her full potential. Unfortunately, our sociological upbringing has, until recently, trained us to believe that the intellect is a man's field, and that a woman's role is to look pretty and make a man happy. Millions of women still need to wake up to the fact that times are thankfully changing, and that they have just as much intelligence and talent as the men in their lives. Because men have a head start in these areas, we often feel frustrated with our intellectual development and end up falling back into this "just a dumb woman" stereotype.

THE SOLUTION

1. Educate yourself. If you know that you haven't been using your intellect as much as you'd like to, decide to change it *now*. Begin by reading—newspapers, quality magazines, books. You don't have to become a scholar. But just knowing what's happening in the world will make you feel more competent. Take classes or seminars to fill in the gaps in your education. Ask lots of questions about things you'd like to understand better. The smarter you feel, the more confidence you'll radiate, and the more turned on your partner will become.

2. Make a list: "The Ways I Play Dumb."

3. Remember: Smart is sexy!

TURN-OFF **16**

Women Who Care Only About a Man's Financial Status

"I can't stand those women who I meet and, right away, they're checking out what kind of car I have, what kind of job I have, what kind of designer clothes I'm wearing, where I take my vacations. I don't feel like they even care about the kind of person I am. All they want is a man to impress their friends, a fancy meal ticket."

"Women say they want a tender, sensitive, open man, one who's willing to work on the relationship, but they really just want a man with money. If a man doesn't have a terrific job, and is only, let's say, a salesperson in a department store, or is just starting his own business, the woman couldn't care less how loving and sweet he is. She's gone, running after some jerk who will treat her like shit, but who drives a Porsche and has a wallet full of credit cards and who can take her to Jamaica for the weekend."

If you ever want to see a man get angry, bring up Turn-off #16. I don't think any other topic elicited more angry responses from the men I interviewed.

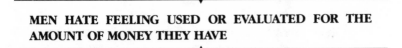

MEN HATE FEELING USED OR EVALUATED FOR THE AMOUNT OF MONEY THEY HAVE

The only feeling I can compare it to is how enraged women get when men use or evaluate us for how big our breasts are, or how perfect our bodies are.

Why This Turns Men Off

Men already walk around feeling pressured to perform. When a woman judges a man purely on his ability to receive financial rewards, he feels totally unappreciated for who he is inside. This lack of emotional safety with a woman is a definite turn-off.

Why Women Do This

Women look at men as "walking bank statements" when:

▼ they look at a man as a "catch" rather than as a human being

▼ they feel they cannot take care of themselves, and must depend on a man to take care of them

▼ they define themselves based on what other people think of the man they "got," rather than on who they are as people.

The Solution

▼

IF YOU WANT MEN TO LOVE YOU FOR WHAT'S INSIDE YOU AND NOT JUST WHAT THEY SEE ON THE OUTSIDE, YOU MUST BE WILLING TO DO THE SAME FOR THEM

▲

In other words, stop evaluating men by their level of success and take a look at the kind of human being they are. There are millions of wonderful, loving, single men who are being overlooked by women because they don't own a fancy car or have a prestigious job or wear flashy clothes. What they have to offer you is much more valuable—sensitivity, fidelity, friendship, and real love.

17

Women Who Use Their Sexuality to Manipulate Men

"Women really turn me off when they put on that 'I'm so hot—come and get me' act. I see this kind of woman in nightclubs all the time. They're hanging out of their clothes, slinking around, looking at me like their body is the bait and I'm the fish they want to catch. I know a lot of men actually respond to this, but they don't respect the women who do it."

"There's a woman at my office who treats men like sexual objects—she flirts, teases, and comes on to them all the time, and then wonders why no one at work takes her seriously."

Men aren't stupid, ladies. They know when a woman is manipulating them with her sexuality. They recognize a sexual tease when they see one. Even though they may appear to love it when you behave that way, even though you may get the attention you want, the men don't respect you, don't take you seriously, and laugh at you behind your back.

The most common ways women do this, however, are much more subtle than the above examples. We act differently around men than the way we act around women. We change our body language for men. We stand a little closer. We move differently. We smile more. We touch more. We throw out unconscious sexual cues in order to get our way with men. I'm not saying women always do this on purpose. We've watched so much of this behavior on television, in the movies, from other women, that we just do it naturally. But these habits limit how you're seen as a woman, and end up undermining your relationships with men.

Why This Turns Men Off

To be accurate, I must say that most men reported that this kind of behavior often turned them on sexually, but turned them off emotionally. One man expressed it like this: "When I see a woman who's obviously trying to look sexy or is coming on strong, I definitely feel my body responding—it's automatic. But it's a physical thing. Inside, I'm feeling disgusted by her and almost humiliated by the way she caused me to respond."

Men know that women are aware of men's sexual vulnerability and how easy it is for them to become physically aroused. Therefore, they resent it when you use this against them, and they end up resenting their own body for responding without their consent. **They feel controlled and overpowered, and this turns them off.**

Why Women Do This

We use our sexuality to manipulate men because we feel powerless. For a long time in our society, sex was the only power women had over men. We had no political power, no economic power, and learned to use sex to get what we wanted. We used it to attract a man, to steal him away from other women, to get him to take care of us, and hopefully, to keep him around. It makes me so sad to see women still behaving as if their only option to feel powerful is to use their sexuality.

The problem with this kind of manipulative behavior is that it works—it works so well that women become trapped in a role they can't escape from. Men don't respect you, and you don't respect yourself.

THE SOLUTION

**IF YOU DON'T WANT TO BE TREATED LIKE A SEX OB-
JECT, DON'T ACT LIKE ONE, AND DON'T TREAT MEN
LIKE ONE**

Take an honest look at your behavior around men. Ask
yourself if you are hiding the real you behind your sexuality.
Try just acting like a person and not a woman. You may not
know what that means until you practice it for a while.

One of the greatest compliments I ever received was
from a well-known TV producer I worked on several projects
with. "You know what I love about you, Barbara?" he said.
"When you're around me, you don't act like a woman, you
act like a person. You deal with me the same way a man
would, and that makes me feel comfortable in your presence
and have a lot of respect for you."

TURN-OFF **18**

Women Who Talk About
Former Lovers

"I've been going out with Suzanne for over a year
now, and she's still talking about her ex-boyfriend. If I
do something better than he did it, she compares us. If
I do something like he did it, she gets angry at me and at
him. I feel like there are three of us in this relationship. I
wish she would have gotten over him completely before we
got together, because it's driving me crazy!"

"I hate it when women bring up their past sexual
experiences. I mean, I don't kid myself that I'm going out

208 ▼ SECRETS ABOUT MEN EVERY WOMAN SHOULD KNOW

with a virgin, but I don't really want to hear about how big or small this other guy's dick was, or even what a lousy lover someone else was. It turns me off to think about all of the men my partner slept with."

It's time to face the truth—your partner doesn't want to hear about the men you've been with before him. He may tolerate it when you bring the subject up, he may even appear curious. But inside, he's turning off. I'm sure you can understand why he wouldn't want to hear you say wonderful things about past lovers, but what about terrible things? Wouldn't those kinds of comments make him feel good? The answer is no!

WHY THIS TURNS MEN OFF

▼ **He decides that you have lousy taste in men.** When you say bad things about your former partners, your man unconsciously thinks, *These guys sound like jerks. Is this the kind of taste in men she has? Does that mean that I'm in the company of jerks? Am I a jerk, and don't know it?*

▼ **He sees the angry, vengeful side of you, and wonders if he's your next target.** When you rant and rave about how terrible your former boyfriend or husband was, you might think your man will feel happy that you dislike your ex so much. But instead, he's coming face to face with the angry, unforgiving part of your personality, and this frightens men. Remember how sensitive they are to criticism. When your partner sees you being that critical, even though it's toward another man, he may unconsciously conclude: *If she can feel this much anger toward someone she used to love, maybe she can do the same with me. Maybe I shouldn't trust her love.*

As one man put it, "Each time my girlfriend rips her ex-husband apart, I feel myself tensing up, even defending the guy. I know her anger toward him is justified, but I guess I'm afraid that she'll turn on me someday."

▼ **He feels angry at you for being such a wimp and letting yourself be mistreated.** "How could my girlfriend be so stupid and let her ex-husband treat her so badly?" one man exclaimed in discussing this turn-off. When you make your ex-partner sound like a monster, it makes your present partner wonder what kind of a woman you are to have let a man so mistreat you.

WHY WOMEN DO THIS

1. We have unresolved feelings about past relationships, and feel safe enough with our present partner to vent those feelings. It's important to heal the anger and blame you carry around inside of you. But the best person to help you work through these emotions may not be your partner. It's easy to make this mistake, especially when you start a new relationship and feel more loved than you ever have before. All that love makes you feel safe enough to open up and release the old pain. You may end up feeling better, but you risk turning your partner off in the process.

2. We use our criticism of former lovers as a sneaky way to tell our new partner how we'd like him to treat us. "I just hated the way Don never bought me little cards or gifts unless it was my birthday. He was so unromantic." A woman makes this remark to her new boyfriend about her former lover. Translation: *Buy me cards and gifts if you know what's good for you!*

▼

WE OFTEN USE THIS FORM OF COVERT COMMUNICATION WITH THE MAN IN OUR LIFE RATHER THAN HAVING AN HONEST CONVERSATION ABOUT WHAT WE WANT AND NEED IN A RELATIONSHIP

▲

The Solution

1. If you have old, unresolved anger and resentment toward former lovers, find a counselor, therapist, or women's support group to help you heal these emotions. This doesn't mean you can't discuss your feelings with your new partner, but *don't use him as an emotional garbage dump.* And remember:

▼

AS LONG AS YOU STILL FEEL ANGER AND BLAME TO-WARD YOUR FORMER PARTNER, YOU ARE ACTUALLY STILL INVOLVED IN A RELATIONSHIP WITH HIM

▲

Your present partner will respect you for healing those negative feelings and will trust you even more than before.

2. Sit down with your partner and discuss your needs and expectations for your relationship. Don't rely on hints, innuendos, or covert communication to ask for what you want. Be honest about your needs and ask your partner to do the same. In Chapter 9 I'll give you some suggestions for creating a new, fulfilling relationship with the man in your life.

TURN-OFF **19** ——————————————

Women Who Aren't Sexually Spontaneous

"The biggest complaint I have about my sex life with my wife is that she always makes such a big deal each time we make love. First of all, she spends at least a half hour in the bathroom washing, putting on body lotion, and who knows what else. Then, she has to set up the bedroom with candles all over the place and the perfect music. By the time she's ready, my interest is gone. I feel like she's getting ready for some kind of performance, and I'm supposed to be the co-star. I mean, sometimes planning it is really nice. But with her, it has to be planned out perfectly or not at all."

"I love spontaneous sex—it's a real turn-on. My last girlfriend and I used to fight about this all the time. We'd come home from working out at our health club, and I'd stop to kiss her at the front door, and I'd say, 'I'm horny, let's make love.' 'Oh, I'm horny, too, honey,' she'd answer, 'but I don't want to do it now—I haven't taken a shower yet, and I still have to pick up our dry cleaning before the party tonight.' She always had some excuse for why it was the wrong time—her hair was still wet from the shower or she was expecting a phone call, or we didn't have enough time. It wasn't that I always wanted it like that—sometimes we'd spend hours making love, and it would be a real ritual. But once in a while, I wished she could just drop everything and say, 'I want you now!' "

We've already discussed some of the reasons men love spontaneous sex: to relieve tension; or because they don't have the energy for a major seduction, but want to unite with you. I heard so many complaints from men about women not being spontaneous enough that I felt it was important to list again as one of the top twenty turn-offs. Especially mentioned were:

▼ women who take forever in the bathroom before they can have sex

▼ women who have to have the perfect lights, music, or setting

▼ women who are worried about how they look—hair, make-up and so on.

Why This Turns Men Off

1. It makes sex a project and puts performance pressure on men. When women prepare for sex as a major undertaking, it sets men up to feel pressured to perform. By now, you should know enough about men to realize that performance pressures turn men off. A friend of mine said it this way, "When a woman can't be spontaneous, she makes sex into an ordeal rather than a spontaneous act of combustion."

2. It makes men feel controlled. Your partner is turned on and wants to make love to you. You agree and disappear into the bathroom for twenty minutes, making him wait for you. How does he feel? *Controlled.* We've seen how feeling controlled turns men off, and this example is no exception.

3. It makes him feel you don't really like sex. When a woman never allows herself to have spontaneous sex, her partner concludes that she must not like sex very much or have that much of a sex drive, since she can exert so much self-control. "My wife can only have sex if she takes the sex out of it," one man confessed to me. He meant that his wife could only have sex if she romanticized it, sanitized it, and idealized it until there was no lust left at all.

Why Women Do This

1. We're afraid of being sexually out of control. As I explained earlier, women are reticent to admit, even to themselves, that they sometimes just want to have lustful sex. So if you catch yourself standing on the stairs with your partner and wanting to do it right then and there, you may feel embarrassed, cheap, or whorish. In other words, you may feel uncomfortable being so sexually out of control. Putting it off until later gives you time to get back in control, even though you'll miss an opportunity for a moment of marvelous passion.

2. It's difficult to be spontaneously lustful toward your partner if you've been feeling emotionally neglected by him. Most women know that we need less physical foreplay if we have been receiving a lot of love, attention, and affection for the days or evening before the actual lovemaking occurs. It's hard to get turned on to your partner if he has hardly touched you all week long and then, when he's suddenly in the mood for sex, expects you to respond with wild abandon. Preparing yourself with a long bath, decorating the room with candles and other nonspontaneous acts are all ways you may be getting yourself in the mood if your partner hasn't done this for you.

THE SOLUTION

Reread Chapter 5 for instructions on how to enjoy spontaneous sex.

TURN-OFF **20**

Women Who Wear Ugly Underwear

"My biggest turn-off of all is when women wear those underpants like my mother wears—the cotton ones that come up to their waist with thick leg parts on the sides. Ugh! I see a pair of those, and I have no interest in what's underneath."

"There's nothing more disgusting than meeting a beautiful woman, going out with her for a while, and finally taking her back to your apartment and undressing her, only to find that she's wearing ratty underwear—saggy underpants, stretched-out, ugly bras. What a disappointment."

I couldn't resist saving this turn-off for last. If you'd have asked me to make a list of the turn-offs I expected men to mention when I interviewed them, I would have never even thought of putting this on the list. And yet you would be amazed at how many men brought this up, and even used the same phrases, including:

▼ "underpants like my mother used to wear"

▼ "saggy underpants that hang down over their ass"

▼ "stretched-out underpants or bras"

▼ "bras that look like chest protectors (the kind with thick backs and lots of hooks)"

▼ "bras that don't fit well (too big or too small)"

Are you as shocked as I was? Did you think men even noticed this stuff? Well, they do, and apparently, when our underwear isn't up to their standards, it's a real turn-off.

Why This Turns Men Off

First of all, anything that reminds a man of his mother (white, baggy underpants; stiff, old-fashioned bras) is a major turn-off for obvious reasons—the old incest taboo. (If she looks too much like Mom, I certainly can't fuck her.) However, the best explanation I heard about this particular turn-off came from a forty-one-year-old writer.

> "When I undress a woman, and notice that she is wearing ugly underwear, it makes me feel three things: *one, that she must not care that much about herself if she can actually wear that stuff; two, that she must not care that much about me to let me see her wearing that stuff; and three, that she must not care that much about sex, because she couldn't possibly feel sexy wearing that* stuff!"

WHY WOMEN DO THIS

What can I say, ladies? Is it because we're lazy, or too cheap to buy ourselves nice undies, or perhaps we had really given up on meeting a man and having sex ever again, and wore those old panties not knowing that a few hours later someone would be looking at them?

THE SOLUTION

Throw out your old, stretched-out, stained underwear. Buy some undies that make you feel beautiful. They don't have to be lace-string-bikini types. There are wonderful all-cotton attractive panties on the market today. And by the way, if your boyfriend or husband is guilty of this same "underwear sin," tell him how much it turns you off, too, and get him to throw out those ripped boxer shorts or stretched-out Jockeys.

Even if you're single, wear underwear that makes you feel sexy. After all, you never know where or when you will meet that right person. I say, be prepared at all times!

I hope you've enjoyed reading this chapter as much as I enjoyed writing it. I suggest that you ask your partner to go through the list and tell you what he thinks about each turn-off. Then, make a list of your own Top Twenty Turnoffs and share it with him. You'll have fun making the list, and your partner will learn as much about you as you just learned about men.

SECRETS

ABOUT

MEN

AND

WOMEN

TOGETHER

7 | *Secrets for Communicating with Men*

Picture this: You arrive in an exotic foreign country where no one speaks any English. But you're not worried—you've come equipped with a special dictionary that explains how to communicate with the natives of this land. You step off the plane and make your first attempt at conversation—using the information in your book—but the person looks at you like you're crazy. You turn to another person and try again, selecting a phrase that your book claims is friendly. This time, the native becomes angry, obviously offended by what you said, and begins to yell at you. Now you're starting to panic, and you frantically search through your book for a sentence to ask for help. You stop and say this sentence to a man on the street, and are amazed to find that, rather than helping you, the man burst into wild laughter and walks away shaking his head. At this point, you realize the terrible truth—*your book is useless.* It's obviously been written for another country entirely, because these people can't understand a word you're saying.

In case you haven't already guessed, this story reflects the frustration women throughout the ages have felt when they try to communicate with the men in their lives. We talk to men in a language we think they are going to understand, only to discover that they don't understand us at all. Can you remember ever having a wonderful discussion with a girl-friend in which she completely comprehended your point of view, and saying to her, "If only I could find a man I could get along with as easily as you, I'd live happily ever after!"

I wrote this chapter to be the guidebook you need to talk to the men you love. It contains secrets about how men think, listen, and express themselves that have been invaluable to me in my life, and I know they'll make an impact on your life as well.

Three Secrets About Communicating with Men

On the following pages, I explain three secrets for understanding men's communication habits. Each secret is divided into three categories of information:

1. What women do wrong in communicating with men based on misunderstanding those habits
2. How men react to what women do wrong
3. Solutions for new ways of communicating

Studying these three secrets and applying the solutions to your life will produce instant results in your relationships with men.

COMMUNICATION
SECRET **1** _____

Men communicate best when they have a focus for the conversation.

Throughout this book we've seen how goal-oriented men are, and how they tend to feel most comfortable operating within boundaries they know about in advance. That way, they can retain a sense of control over whatever situation they're in. For this reason, men need to have a focus in mind when they have a conversation with you. They like to know what the purpose of the discussion is and what you want from them. This gives them the sense that they know what they're doing when they are talking with you.

WHAT WOMEN DO WRONG:

We are too vague in our requests for communication. We say:

"Let's have a talk."
"Honey, I think we should discuss our relationship."
"Help me figure out what to do about my job."

The problem with these comments are that they are too vague, unfocused, and open-ended. They don't give your partner any kind of direction to take, or any boundaries within which the discussion can develop. This will make him very uncomfortable, as if he's now supposed to figure out what you want and need from him. He feels out of control. He feels pressured to perform, but he doesn't know the rules of the game, and this creates fear and uncertainty.

Most women don't have this problem. That's because:

▼

WOMEN ARE MORE PROCESS ORIENTED THAN GOAL ORIENTED
▲

Two girlfriends can sit down together and say "let's talk," and it doesn't bother them a bit that they have no idea where the conversation is going or what the purpose of it is. They enjoy the process of just expressing themselves. But many men find this lack of structure very disconcerting.

How Men React

Your partner may act uninterested in pursuing the conversation.

He may appear resistant to talking with you.

He may become argumentative in an attempt to dissuade you from persisting.

He may keep putting off having the talk you want.

He may think you are spaced out or don't know what you want to say, and won't take you seriously.

The Solution

1. When you want to have a discussion with a man, give him an agenda. Tell him exactly what you'd like to talk about, what you hope to accomplish, and what you expect from him. For instance:

> "Honey, let's spend time just talking tonight. We haven't really had any time together since your mother visited us last week. Why don't you tell me what you thought of the visit, and I'll tell you how it felt to me. That way, we will know how to handle things even better next time she comes."

> "Jim, I'd like to talk with you about our relationship. We've been going out for six months, and I thought this would be a good time for us to evaluate our strengths and weaknesses. I know this would make me feel more secure, and give me a better idea of what parts of the relationship need work."

> "Harry, I really need your help in figuring out how to handle my boss. I've been feeling very overworked lately, and I'm starting to resent it. I'm not sure how to approach him about it, and I thought if I got a man's opinion, I'd make a better decision."

In each of these examples, the woman gave her partner a *focus* for the conversation, rather than just saying: "Let's talk about your mother's visit," or "Let's discuss our relationship," or "I need your help with my job." Now the man has a *goal* in mind for the discussion, and feels more comfortable entering into it.

2. Ask him questions. Asking a man questions also helps structure a conversation for him. The more specific the question, the better. For instance:

▼

Wrong way: "How's work?"

Your partner will give you the briefest possible answer, such as, "Fine."

Right way: "Honey, how are you doing with that new project at work? Is it as tough as you thought it would be?"

▲

▼

Wrong way: "Jim, I think we should talk about our relationship."

Jim will feel put on the spot and probably respond, "Why, is something wrong?"

Right way: "Jim, I think we should talk about our relationship. We've been dating for six months now. What do you think our strengths and weaknesses are, and in what direction would you like to see us go?"

▲

▼

Wrong way: "Harry, I need your help with my boss."

Harry will feel as if you're asking him to find a solution to a problem by himself, and will instantly feel overwhelmed.

Right way: "Harry, I'm having a problem with my boss at work. [Explain problem.] Do you think I should confront him directly, or go through my supervisor? How would you handle it?"

▲

3. Don't use hinting as a way to ask for what you want—be direct. One of the worst habits we have as women is not being direct in our communication with the men in our lives: *hinting* about something we want, instead of asking for it; *testing* our partner by asking him what he thinks about an issue rather than taking the risk of sharing our own opinion; *being vague* about what's bothering us rather than coming right out and talking about it. All these tactics make men feel very manipulated, and that makes them angry.

"I can't stand when my wife hints around about something," one husband told me. "I know what she's trying to say, but the way she does it makes me feel she thinks I'm stupid enough to fall for it, or wimpy enough that she can manipulate me. I wish she'd just come out and say what's on her mind."

Take this man's advice—be direct with the men in your life. That way they'll know what your agenda is and feel safer in communicating with you.

COMMUNICATION
SECRET **2** _____

Men internalize their thinking process and only communicate the end result.

By now you know that men have been trained to have all the answers and not show their fear or uncertainty. The result is that men frequently internalize their thinking process, and wait to express themselves until they've come up with a conclusion or a solution. One man I know calls this process "mulling." Men "mull" things over silently. Don't forget:

▼
MEN ARE SOLUTION ORIENTED
▲

Men prefer expressing themselves only when they know the answer or solution, and not before. They do their thinking and figuring out silently. This is why, if you ask your partner for his advice, or a question about your relationship, he may respond by saying "Let me think about it." He doesn't want to give a quick answer that may be "wrong." In fact, when I interviewed men for this book, the majority of them felt very put on the spot when I expected them to answer immediately, and said, "Let me think about it."

WHAT WOMEN DO WRONG

We think out loud.

"I hate when my wife opens her mouth and every thought in her head starts pouring out."

"You know what drives me crazy? When women start going through every step of a problem out loud, listing all the possibilities, or everything they need to do that day. It makes me want to run out of the room."

I heard these and other, similar comments countless times as I interviewed men. The problem again lies in the differences between men and women, and in the fact that men are solution oriented while women are process oriented. Look at the difference in how a man and a woman express the same information.

Judy talking to her husband Bob: "Let's see. I'm going to take your suit to the cleaner's this morning, I meant to drop it off yesterday, but I got caught up at that meeting until after six. Then, I guess since I'll be so close by, I'll drop in to the department store and see if I can return that pair of slacks I bought last week—you know, the ones that have the little spot on the front. Actually, maybe I should go to the store first, since it will be less crowded, and then go to the cleaner's. That will work better—it's so hard to park at the mall when it's packed. Oh, I almost forgot, I promised Cindy I'd get her the number of that massage therapist. I'd better go write it down. I wonder where I left my appointment book. Honey, have you seen my calendar anywhere? Let's see, the last time I had it was when I was on the phone in the kitchen. . . .

Bob talking to his wife Judy: "Honey, I have a bunch of errands to do this morning, so I'll see you later."

Are you as embarrassed as I am reading this? What's happening here is:

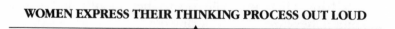

WOMEN EXPRESS THEIR THINKING PROCESS OUT LOUD

We don't even realize we do this. Judy isn't really trying to communicate all that information to Bob. It's just that it's easier for her to think about her day when she goes through it step by step and hears herself talking. Bob is left sitting there and feeling what most men end up feeling.

HOW MEN REACT

Most men react just like Bob reacts as he sits there listening to Judy. They think, **Women talk too much!**

What men really mean when they say this is that women share more of their thoughts and feelings with men than men want to hear. To us, it's normal; to most men, it's excessive.

"GET TO THE POINT"

Have you ever been trying to express your feelings to your partner, and you notice him squirming around in his chair, looking impatient, until he finally looks up and says, "Honey, would you please get to the point?" You end up feeling like he isn't listening to you and doesn't care about your emotions, and he ends up feeling like you are torturing him on purpose!

Perhaps you can understand this common dilemma a little better now that you know how solution oriented men are. They want the bottom line on how you are feeling in twenty-five words or less. What men don't understand is that the very process of talking about feelings is part of what helps resolve those feelings and give you more insight and clarity into the problem.

WHAT WOMEN DO WRONG:

Women complain out loud about their problems without letting the man know we feel hopeful about finding a solution.

This is why men accuse women of whining and complaining a lot. Although some women do play the victim and complain, but do nothing about making changes in their lives, others of us do take charge of our problems. However, women often "complain out loud" about what's bothering them, while men often internalize their complaining.

How Men React

When a man hears his wife running out her negative thoughts about something, he doesn't understand that this is her way of releasing her mental tension. He doesn't understand that she's actually making progress toward resolving her dilemma.

> He *becomes impatient,* assuming she's going on and on because she can't find a solution.
> He ends up *feeling responsible* for fixing things for her.
> He *tries to rush her* through to the solution of her problems.

The Solution

1. Discuss this secret with the man in your life. Explain your way of thinking and talking to him, and let him know you understand his way too. I've done this in my own relationship, and now whenever I start thinking out loud, my partner looks at me and we both start to laugh. I'm not saying you should stop thinking out loud if you enjoy doing it, but discussing this with your partner will make things easier for both of you.

2. When discussing a problem with your partner, give him time to come up with an answer. Let's say you and your husband are planning a trip next month, and you want to talk about whether you should leave on Thursday night or Friday morning.

▼

Wrong way: **Start talking out loud about every possibility, and its pros and cons, and pressure your partner into giving you his answer immediately.**

Right way: **Present the information to your partner and say, "Do you want to talk about this now, or would you rather think about it for a while and let me know your answer later?"**

▲

This gives your partner an opportunity to mull over the information without feeling put on the spot or fearful that he might give the wrong answer. Giving your partner the option to discuss the problem now or later also gives him a sense of personal choice and freedom, and avoids bringing out the rebel in him, who may feel controlled if you demand an immediate response.

3. Let your partner know when you need to complain out loud in order to solve a problem, so that he is warned in advance! As I've said, men will usually feel obliged to rescue you if they hear you complaining without an apparent direction. Tell your partner when you're in the mood to complain out loud. Let him know you are interested in finding a solution, and that this is your way of working through your mental confusion toward some clarity.

COMMUNICATION SECRET **3**

Men don't have access to their emotions as easily as women do.

"It drives me crazy when I know something is bothering my husband, and when I ask him what's wrong, he answers,

'Nothing.' Why is it so hard for him to get in touch with his feelings?"

"My boyfriend and I get into fights all the time over the same thing. I'll want to discuss something about our relationship and he doesn't want to talk about it. I'll pour my heart out to him, and he will sit there listening and not responding. I end up screaming at him that he's a cold, unemotional bastard, and we have a huge argument."

Here's a very important secret about men that you need to know: **To most men, the inner world of emotions is a strange and frightening place.**

▼ **The emotional world is unfamiliar.** Most men have been conditioned to stay in their heads, and not in their hearts, so they aren't used to spending a lot of time delving into their feelings. Remember:

▼

HUMAN BEINGS FEEL COMFORTABLE WITH WHAT THEY ARE MOST FAMILIAR WITH

▲

And we've seen that, based on our socialization process, women are more familiar with feelings than men. No one likes to spend time doing something they are uncomfortable with. No one enjoys doing something they aren't good at.

If you have a lot of confidence in your knowledge of modern art, then you probably enjoy talking about it with people. If you have no experience with investing in tax-free bonds, you have little confidence in that field, and don't enjoy talking about it.

Since men don't have a lot of confidence in their emotional ability, it's no surprise that men don't enjoy examining or expressing their feelings as much as we'd like them to.

▼ **Visiting the emotional world makes men feel out of control.** When men don't feel they are good at something, they feel controlled by it, as if it has power over them, rather than their having power over it. This sense of being out of control is frightening to men, and they avoid it at all costs. Therefore, men tend to avoid the world of emotions, since they lack the emotional fluency with which they feel they can master it.

Have you ever been really out of shape physically and thought about going for a hike or taking an aerobics class? Not a very appealing idea, is it? That's because you'd be forced to do an activity you aren't skilled at, one that will be a strain for you. Well, apply this analogy to men and their resistance to talking about their feelings. The truth is:

▼

MOST MEN ARE EMOTIONALLY OUT OF SHAPE
▲

Therefore, indulging in emotional exercises, such as talking about feelings, expressing their doubts and worries, even asking for what they need is a strain for many men, just as that five-mile hike would be a strain for you if you weren't in shape.

WHAT WOMEN DO WRONG

1. We misinterpret men's lack of familiarity with feeling as stubborn resistance, and blame them for being "insensitive."

The majority of the men I interviewed expressed anger and hurt at how frequently women label men "insensitive, unfeeling, unemotional." It's important to understand that male insensitivity is a myth.

▼

MEN ARE JUST AS SENSITIVE, AND IN SOME WAYS MORE SENSITIVE, THAN WOMEN ARE

▲

Men don't always have easy access to their feelings. *So while it looks as if they aren't feeling anything, the truth is that they just aren't in touch with what they are feeling.* So when you ask your partner, "What are you feeling?" rather than risk sounding stupid or admit that he doesn't know what he's feeling (Remember: Saying "I don't know" is difficult for men), he may answer: "Nothing."

2. We expect men to be able to get in touch with their feelings as quickly as we can. Not all, but most women are more emotionally fluent than most men, because we've had longer to practice. It's a mistake to expect your partner to be able to figure out what he's feeling in a few minutes, always recognize his buried emotions, and comfortably share his fears and vulnerabilities with you as well as you do with him. I'm not saying that men are incapable of becoming emotionally masterful. Over the past ten years I've worked with thousands of men through my Making Love Work seminars who wanted to learn how to master the world of the heart, and I have seen them grow into very loving, emotionally expressive human beings. It takes retraining, practice, and the everyday use of tools and techniques for both men and women to get rid of old emotional habits and create new, healthy ones.

3. We assume that intellectually articulate men will be emotionally articulate. Have you ever met a man who is successful, well educated, and highly intelligent, and because he is so articulate in other areas, you assume he's going to be emotionally expressive as well? I went out with a man like this once. I met him at a conference where he was one of the speakers. He spoke eloquently, with great sensitivity, and was very knowledgeable about philosophy, psychology, and spirituality. "Here's a guy I could really fall in love with!" I said to myself. "He seems so sensitive, so expressive."

The first few times we went out, I felt excited about the prospect of having a relationship with this man. We would go to dinner, and have wonderful intellectual discussions about the meaning of life. He would quote poetry to me. Everything seemed fine. But after three or four dates, I began to notice something strange. This man never talked about *how he felt.* He would give me his opinions or his intellectual analysis, but not his feelings. It didn't take long for me to realize that although he was comfortable talking from his head, he was very uncomfortable talking from his heart. In fact, as he admitted to me later, one of the reasons he appeared to be such an intellectual was that he used what he knew to avoid what he felt.

▼

DON'T BE FOOLED BY AN ARTICULATE, WELL-SPOKEN MAN, HE MAY REALLY BE A FRIGHTENED LITTLE BOY INSIDE WHO HAS A HARD TIME EXPRESSING THE SIMPLEST EMOTIONS

▲

HOW MEN REACT

When you judge men for not being as emotionally developed as you are, they end up feeling criticized and misunderstood and will retaliate by becoming even more resistant to giving you the kind of emotional responses you want. They become:

▼ rebellious

▼ uncooperative when it comes to having conversations

▼ angry at you and prone to attacking you as being too emotional

---

SOMETIMES, WHEN A MAN ISN'T SURE OF WHAT HE'S FEELING, AND YOU ARE PRESSURING HIM TO TALK TO YOU, HE WILL CHANGE THE SUBJECT, OR VERBALLY ATTACK YOU, HOPING TO BUY TIME TO FIGURE OUT WHAT'S GOING ON INSIDE HIM

How Kelly and Michael Learned to Argue Less and Love More

Kelly and Michael were a young, married couple who came to me because they were fighting too much of the time. "We always go through the same thing," Kelly complained. "I want to talk to Michael about our relationship. Maybe something is bothering me, or I'm not feeling like I'm getting enough attention, or whatever it is. So I bring the subject up, and no matter what it is, Michael tries to avoid the discussion. He tries to convince me that I'm upset over nothing, or starts asking me a lot of questions about myself and putting me on the hot spot, or he attacks me for being such an "emotional basket case." I end up feeling that he doesn't want to work on the relationship at all, and wonder why I even married him in the first place."

I asked Kelly if I could speak to Michael alone. "Michael, tell me what goes on inside of you when Kelly tries to get you involved in an emotional discussion."

"Well," Michael replied quietly, "I know that right away, I feel uncomfortable. I'm not sure what she expects of me. The fact that she even wants to talk to me makes me feel like I did something wrong. And she talks so fast and throws so much information at me, I can't really take it all in. I start feeling really overwhelmed, like I wish things would slow down."

"How do you feel when Kelly asks you to talk about your feelings?"

Michael paused for a moment and then answered,

"Pressured—like I might make a mistake. Confused—because I feel put on the spot to figure out how I'm feeling, and I'm not always sure of it. It's as if Kelly wants to have an answer ready right then, and when I don't, I feel really uptight."

"So what do you need from her when this happens?"

"Well," Michael replied, "I guess I need more time, just to have her back off a little bit and let me think about what she said, and figure out how I feel."

"And do you ask her for that time? Do you tell her that you feel pressured and uncomfortable?"

"Not really." Michael shook his head. "I've never really been in touch with it until right now. I end up just acting like a jerk, to tell you the truth. I get real sarcastic, or angry, and make her feel like she's the one with the problem. I guess I'm trying to intimidate her into dropping the whole thing so I can get a hold of myself and come up with an answer."

Michael was a perfect example of a man who wasn't emotionally articulate, who avoided emotional discussions with his wife to cover up his own feelings of inadequacy and frustration at not always being able to express his feelings. When Kelly came back into the room, I explained Michael's behavior to her, and she was very relieved. "I thought Michael didn't love me enough," she confessed. "But now I understand that he wasn't avoiding me because of lack of love, but because he felt so uncomfortable being put on the spot." Kelly agreed to try the suggestions I list below, and Michael agreed to be honest with Kelly whenever he was feeling like he needed time to mull over his feelings. The last time I spoke with them they reported that their whole style of communicating with one another has changed for the better.

THE SOLUTION

1. Don't overwhelm your partner with your emotions by pouring them out all at once and expecting him to respond. Slow down—take your time—be clear about

what you want to say. If you were speaking English to someone from another country who was just learning our language, you'd talk very slowly and clearly, wouldn't you? I'm not saying you should talk to a man as if he's illiterate, but it does help to take your time, to be clear about what you want to say rather than rambling on and on with no direction. This will prevent your partner from becoming overwhelmed, and give him time to access his feelings. It's okay for there to be periods of silence—don't fill them all up with words.

▼

SOMETIMES WHEN YOUR PARTNER IS SILENT, HE'S NOT IGNORING YOU—HIS MIND IS PROCESSING THE INFORMATION YOU GAVE HIM, AND HE'S TRYING TO GET IN TOUCH WITH HIS FEELINGS

▲

▼

Wrong way: Accuse him of being emotionally retarded, insist that he finish the conversation now whether he likes it or not, follow him around the house yelling at him until he answers you, cry and blame him for rejecting you.

Right way: "Look, I know I said a lot just now, and it's probably a little overwhelming. Why don't we take a break, so we can both think about how we feel, and talk again in a little while? I love you, and I know we can work this out."

▲
---

2. Try physically touching your partner, holding hands, resting your hand on his arm, or hugging him as a way to help him get out of his head and into his heart.

A COMMUNICATION CHART

Here's a chart to help you study these three secrets about communicating with men.

Secret	What Women Do Wrong	How Men React	Solution
1. Men communicate best when they have a focus for the conversation—they are goal oriented.	We are vague and unfocused—we are process oriented.	They act disinterested. They become resistant. They don't take you seriously.	Give your man an agenda. Ask him questions.
2. Men internalize their thinking process and only communicate the end result—they are solution oriented.	We think out loud. We complain without sharing our hopeful feelings.	They think women talk too much. They become impatient and try to rush you. They feel responsible.	Discuss your style of communicating with your partner. Give him time to come up with an answer. Warn him if you need to complain.
3. Men don't have access to their emotions as easily as women do—it's unfamiliar territory.	We blame men for being insensitive. We expect men to be able to feel their emotions as quickly as we can. We assume that intellectually articulate men will be emotionally articulate.	They feel criticized and misunderstood. They rebel. They verbally attack you.	Go slowly when expressing your feelings. Make your partner feel safe; he doesn't have to do it perfectly. Acknowledge him for his progress. Give him time to explore his feelings. Be affectionate.

This is one of the quickest and sometimes the simplest way to help the man you love get in touch with his feelings. Men are very identified with their bodies, and your physical touch will pull your partner out of his purely logical, analytical, and unemotional thinking patterns into a more sensitive, vulnerable state.

▼

WHEN YOU NOTICE THAT YOUR PARTNER IS HAVING A DIFFICULT TIME EXPRESSING HIS FEELINGS OR LISTENING TO YOURS, ASK TO HOLD HIM FOR A MOMENT IN SILENCE

▲

This can shift the energy of your conversation in just a few moments from an intellectual battle to a loving exchange.

How to Listen to Men

Have you ever been having a discussion with the man you love and felt you were right there for him, only to have him turn to you angrily and yell: "You're not listening to me."?

Do you ever get impatient with your partner when he's trying to express himself, and feel that it's taking him forever to say what he needs to say?

One of the biggest complaints men have about us is that *women don't know how to listen.*

I know that when I used to hear a partner tell me this, it would drive me crazy. "What do you mean, I don't listen?" I'd ask defensively. "I'm sitting here with you. I haven't gone anywhere." It's taken me years to understand how men need to be listened to so they feel heard. Here are some listening tips that you can begin to practice in your own life.

LISTENING
TIP 1

Don't Interrupt a Man When He Is Trying to Express Himself

"You're interrupting me again!" How many times have you heard that from a man during a discussion? My response to this used to be: "I'm not interrupting, I'm telling you how I feel, too. What do you want me to do, just sit here and say nothing and let you talk?" If men were honest, their answer would be, "Yes, that's exactly what I'd like you to do." We think they don't want to hear what we have to say. But that's usually not why men don't like being interrupted. Here are some other reasons to consider:

▼ **Men need to concentrate when they are trying to access their emotions.** By now you should understand how much more of an effort it takes for a man to talk about his feelings than it takes most women. And you recall that men have difficulty doing two things at once. When you put these two facts together, you can see why men hate being interrupted during a discussion or argument.

▼

WHEN YOU INTERRUPT A MAN DURING A CONVERSATION, IT TEMPORARILY DISTRACTS HIM FROM STAYING FOCUSED ON HIS FEELINGS

▲

If your partner is trying to sort through his feelings, a skill most men are still developing, and you start talking back to him, it breaks his concentration. You're simply trying to make a point, but by stopping his own thought process and listening to you, your partner becomes distracted from his focus, and this makes him irritated and angry.

▼ **Men are goal oriented, so when they begin a thought, they like to complete it.** I know it doesn't bother you to start a conversation on one topic, shift to another, leave both of those and go in a completely new direction, and finally return to the original subject, but this drives men crazy! Remember, men are much more goal oriented than women are, *so men tend to think in a straight line, or in a more linear fashion, than in a spiral as women frequently do.* So when your partner wants to go from point A to point B in a discussion, and you interrupt with points C, D, and E, you are pulling him off his purpose. He doesn't see this as you contributing to the discussion—he sees it as an obstacle to the achievement of his goal.

▼ **Men need to feel they are doing it right, and they interpret interruption as your way of saying "You're doing it wrong."** When a man expresses himself, he's not only interested in getting what is inside him out, but in doing it "right," whatever that means to him. Believe it or not, men are more careful about what they say than women are, and although what you're hearing may not make much sense to you, your man is putting a lot of effort into it. So when you interrupt him in the middle of his communication attempts, he interprets this as your saying: "You aren't doing it right, so I'm going to stop you right now before you get any worse," kind of like the *Gong Show* on television, where the performers who are doing a terrible job are "gonged" off the stage.

THE SOLUTION

------------------------------▼------------------------------

LISTEN TO YOUR PARTNER WITHOUT INTERRUPTING HIM

------------------------------▲------------------------------

This means that, if your partner wants to discuss something with you, let him express himself, and wait until he is completely finished before you respond.

▼

Important: Don't leap in the moment your partner takes a breath or pauses, claiming, "Oh, I thought you were done."

▲

Make sure he has said everything he wants to by asking,

> "Is there anything else you need to tell me?"
> or
> "What else would you like to say about this?"

Then, when he feels complete, you can have your chance to express your feelings. Of course, you should insist that he doesn't interrupt you either. This doesn't mean that every time you talk, you need to take turns giving long discourses. But especially during the initial expression of feelings, or introduction of a subject, this will be a helpful tip to remember.

LISTENING
TIP **2**

Be Patient While He Explores His Emotions

In my book *How to Make Love All the Time,* I talk about the "Emotional Map," a powerful yet simple formula to help you understand your own feelings and the feelings of others, and to assist you in moving out of unpleasant emotions, such as anger, hurt, or fear, and back to a state of love. According to the Emotional Map, whenever you feel upset or emotionally off balance you are experiencing five levels of emotion at the same time. These levels are:

The Emotional Map

1. *Anger,* blame, and resentment
2. *Hurt,* sadness, and disappointment
3. *Fear,* worry, and insecurity
4. *Remorse,* regrets, and responsibility
5. *Love,* understanding, appreciation, and forgiveness

When something upsets you, you usually experience the emotions closest to the surface, like anger or hurt. But like the floors of a building, our emotions build, one layer on top of the next. Anger, blame, and resentment are the first layer; they are the way we protect ourselves when we feel attacked or unloved. Underneath lies hurt, sadness, and disappoint-ment—much more vulnerable emotions. The hurt covers up the even more vulnerable feelings of fear, worry, and insecu-rity. As you move away from these intense feelings, and get closer to the core, you are able to feel remorse and regrets, and can take responsibility for understanding the real truth about what you're experiencing. And underneath all the anger, hurt, fear, and remorse is love. The other emotions are simply reactions we go through when something interferes with our ability to feel loved or loving.

Taking an Elevator from Your Head to Your Heart

I have an analogy I use in my seminars about taking an elevator down from our head into our heart, from the top floor of our emotions—anger and blame—down to the bottom floor—love and understanding. Each time you choose to explore your emotions and look at what I call the Complete Truth (all five levels) about how you feel, you have to start at the top and work your way down. Using the Emotional Map, you begin to express your upset feelings of anger and take your elevator down, stopping on each "floor" to express that layer of emotion, until you're at the ground floor of love.

▼

**LEARNING TO MASTER EXPRESSING YOUR EMOTIONS
MEANS KNOWING HOW TO GET INTO THAT ELEVATOR
AND TAKE IT DOWN THROUGH ALL THE LEVELS OF
FEELING, COMMUNICATING THE COMPLETE TRUTH TO
YOURSELF AND YOUR PARTNER AS YOU GO**

▲

In my work with people I've found that, for all the
reasons we discussed earlier in the book, most men have a
slower elevator than most women. This means that it takes
them longer to get in touch with what they are feeling
underneath their initial reaction of anger, discomfort, or
irritation.

This is why women become impatient with men when
men try to communicate their feelings. It's not that they're
trying to irritate you. It's not that they're dumb. It's not that
they're being resistant. Men simply take longer to figure out
what they are feeling, because they are more unfamiliar with
that inner world than women are.

How I Broke My Bad Listening Habits

One of the biggest listening mistakes we make with the
men in our lives is being impatient with their process. This
used to be a bad habit I had with men, and being a therapist
made it even worse. I'd be sitting with a partner, and he'd be
trying to tell me something that was bothering him. By the
time he'd said four or five sentences about it, I'd already sped
way past him, figured out what he was really feeling, and had
my answer ready. He'd still be talking, but I'd sit there
squirming, wondering how long it was going to take him to
get it, until I couldn't stand it anymore. Then, I'd interrupt
and say something like, "Honey, here's what I think is happening," and I'd lay the whole thing out for him. Now I must
admit, most of the time I was right in my assessment of his

emotions, but by putting words in his mouth, I didn't give him an opportunity to feel his own feelings and complete his own process. He'd end up feeling angry, ripped off, mothered, and put down.

One day, after I had just delivered what I felt was a brilliant analysis of my partner's feelings, he blurted out just what I needed to hear: "Look, Barbara," he said. "Maybe I can't think as fast as you can or figure out how I'm feeling as quickly as you do. This is all still new for me, okay. I know you're trying to be helpful, but *let me do it myself!"*

As much as I hated hearing this, I knew my partner was right. The point of our conversation wasn't for me to figure out what he wanted to tell me, but for him to figure out what he wanted to tell me. My impatience was preventing him from participating 100 percent in his own emotional process. How was he ever going to learn to express himself completely if I always rushed in and did it for him? It would be like your thinking you were helping your child with his arithmetic by giving him the answers—he'd never learn to solve the problems by himself.

THE SOLUTION

1. Give your partner permission to be emotionally inarticulate. The language of emotion is usually a second language to men and a first language for women. Don't expect your partner to be as emotionally fluent as you are. Give him time during a discussion or argument to explore his own feelings, even though you may think you know what the real problem is. Appreciate his willingness to go through the process of emotionally revealing himself, even if he takes longer at it than you would.

2. Introduce him to the Emotional Map, and help lead him through the five levels of feeling. If you are serious about making your relationship even better, read *How to Make Love All the Time* with your partner, and practice the techniques that will help you develop good communication skills that you can use both personally and professionally. You can help your partner out when he seems to be stumbling in his attempts to express himself by asking him questions that will take him through those five levels of feeling:

"What are you angry at me (or whomever) about?"
"What did I (or someone else) do that hurt you?"
"What's making you sad right now?"
"What are you disappointed about?"
"What are you afraid might happen?"
"What are you worried about?"

Let him figure out how to say "I'm sorry" and "I love you" by himself! And don't start interrogating him as soon as he opens his mouth. Give him time to find his own way, and point him in the right direction if he seems lost.

3. Make sure you are using your own Emotional Map when you express yourself to your partner. It's no fair expecting your partner to play by the rules when you get to break them. Make sure to practice what you preach. The more you demonstrate how positive, complete, and loving good communication is, the more you will set an example for your partner to follow.

LISTENING
TIP **3**

Let Your Partner Know You Understand His Point of View

There's almost nothing that gets men more agitated than feeling misunderstood. Often they feel this way because we don't acknowledge their feelings as they express them to us.

▼

MEN WILL BE MUCH MORE WILLING TO RESPECT YOUR FEELINGS IF YOU SHOW THEM THAT YOU UNDERSTAND THEIRS

▲

Here are some ways to give men positive feedback when you are listening to them.

1. Practice active listening—duplicate what you hear them say. This is a simple communication technique therapists teach couples to help them learn to listen to one another more effectively. After listening to your partner express himself, rephrase what you think he said to you and say it back to him:

▼

Ted: "Mary, I'm really feeling frustrated lately with what's going on in our sex life. It seems like you're never in the mood for sex, and I don't know if it's me or if it's something else, but I'm starting to feel really distant from you, and I don't want to feel that way. You keep giving me excuses, like the kids are bugging you, or you're too tired, or you have a headache, but it's been three weeks since we've made love, and I think something else must be going on. I know we haven't spent much time together lately, so maybe you aren't feeling close, I don't know, I just hate it this way."

Mary (poor listening): "How can you say that? I've hardly seen you this month, you've been so damn busy. You're the one who comes home at night exhausted. Do you think that turns me on? You don't know what it's like to have a new baby and two other kids to raise."

Mary (good listening): "So you feel like I am rejecting you, and maybe don't like having sex with you? That

must feel awful, and kind of scary, especially when I know how affectionate you are."

Ted: **"Yes, I do, and it hurts."**

▲

When Ted feels that Mary has acknowledged his initial feelings, he feels safe to go on and explore his emotions more deeply. Now he can follow that Emotional Map down from anger into more vulnerable feelings like hurt and fear.

2. Give men visual and verbal cues that indicate you are listening to and understanding them. If you are listening to your partner but you're sitting there silently staring back at him, you can be sure he will feel like you aren't listening to him. Men need a lot of encouragement for entering the realm of their emotions. There are several ways you can give your partner this support:

▼ Remember, men are visually oriented. So if you nod your head as your partner makes a point, he will feel accepted and heard.

▼ Saying "uh-huh" or "hmmm" lets your partner know you are listening and understand what he is trying to say to you. You don't have to agree with what he is saying, but you can still acknowledge that you understand.

LISTENING
TIP **4**

Touch Your Partner

Remember: Physical touch helps your partner stay connected with you and allows him to feel more of his feelings. Don't overdo it, but as I said earlier in this chapter, holding hands, sitting close together, or resting your hand on your partner's arm will create more intimacy and promote a more emotionally satisfying conversation.

These listening tips have worked really well for me, and I hope they work for you too. Be sure to share this information with your partner so he can also become a great listener.

Five of the Most Commonly Asked Questions About How Men Communicate

Here are five questions I hear over and over again from women wanting to know about how men communicate. Understanding the answers to these questions will help you create much more rewarding relationships with the men in your life.

1. WHY DOES THE MAN IN MY LIFE ALWAYS TRY TO TALK ME OUT OF MY FEELINGS WHEN WE ARE HAVING A FIGHT?

Have you ever been trying to express your feelings to the man you love—about something you're not happy with; something you need from him that you're not getting; something he did that hurt you—maybe you're even in tears, and somehow, within a few minutes, you find yourself in the middle of a heated intellectual debate, and you're losing? You can't figure out what happened. You started out feeling very emotional and vulnerable, and ended up defensive and sarcastic.

You've been an unsuspecting victim of a tactic men use when they feel threatened, frightened or vulnerable: *They try to talk you out of your feelings.*

▼

WHEN MEN FEEL THREATENED OR AFRAID, THEY WILL TRY TO GET YOU OUT OF YOUR HEART AND INTO YOUR HEAD SO THEY CAN WIN AN ARGUMENT AND STAY IN CONTROL

▲

Men feel much more at home operating from their intellects than they do from their hearts—they have more practice. So when you instigate an emotional exchange, your partner feels you have an immediate advantage over him. In order to shift the balance of power to his side, your man will attempt to steer the conversation away from feelings and over to the facts. He'll ask you lots of questions; he'll make observations rather than share his emotions; he'll try to make you doubt your own feelings by saying things like:

▼ "You sound neurotic—you're getting to be an emotional basket case."

▼ "I can't believe you're falling apart like this."

▼ "Calm down—you're getting hysterical."

▼ "You are so hypersensitive and needy."

Most women fall for this tactic, disconnect from how they feel, and *get lured into an intellectual battle with their partner*. This way he is likely to win (especially if he is an attorney!) or at least he won't feel like he lost. The original problem doesn't get resolved, you walk away frustrated and confused, and he walks away relieved that he avoided being confronted on his emotional inadequacies. Although some men aren't aware of this habit, the majority of men I interviewed are totally conscious when they do this with women.

The Solution: Don't let him get away with it! **Stay in your heart, in touch with how you feel**—that's where you are most powerful as a woman. Inform your partner that you're on to his tricks, and that they won't work anymore. And remember—avoiding the real issues isn't any more fulfilling for your partner than it is for you. The safer a man feels working with his emotions, the less threatened he'll be when you need to talk.

2. WHY DO MEN HATE TALKING ABOUT EMOTIONAL ISSUES LATE AT NIGHT?

It's 11:15 at night. You and your partner are lying in bed reading. You've had something on your mind all day that you want to discuss with your partner, so you turn to him and say, "Honey, could we talk a little bit?" Your partner looks at you with about as much enthusiasm as a slug and responds, "It's awfully late, isn't it? Couldn't it wait until the morning?" When you persist, he either gets angry at you, and makes comments like:

▼ "Why do you always wait until late at night to bring things up?"

▼ "You know it's never a short discussion—you'll end up going on and on."

▼ "Can't I have a little peace and quiet at the end of the day?"

▼ "Why do we always have to talk about things when you want to?"

or he agrees to listen, and:

▼ falls asleep during the conversation

▼ acts unresponsive to your thoughts and feelings

▼ answers in mono-syllabic grunts and groans

Why does discussing emotional issues late at night bother many men so much?

1. Men feel less in control late at night when they are tired. Men often look at a conversation as a mini–power struggle. When the conversation is emotional in content, men already feel at a disadvantage, as we've seen before. So your partner will try to postpone having a discussion when he's feeling fatigued, because he knows he isn't going to be able to feel in control as much as he'd like to. Of course, the opposite is true for women—we instinctively like talking to men when they're tired, because their resistance is lower and their mind isn't as sharp.

2. Men fear you will go on and on and they won't get any sleep. This goes back to our communication secret about men needing to have an agenda in order to feel comfortable with a conversation. When it's late at night, and you want to have a talk, and a man knows he's your captive audience, a fear rises up within him that says: *She'll start talking and never stop. We'll be up all night; I'll be exhausted for work tomorrow; I'll make mistakes on the job. I'll get fired. I'll be a failure. Well, that settles it, no discussion tonight!*

The Solution: **Discuss this issue with your partner, and make some agreements about late-night discussions.** You may need to compromise sometimes and wait until the next morning. You might also try giving your partner a time limit: "Honey, I need to talk with you. Can you give me fifteen minutes? I know you're tired, but that will help me feel better, and we can continue when you have more time."

Make sure you don't hold in your negative feelings for days and weeks, and then dump them all on your partner late one night. Naturally, he'll feel overwhelmed. Always discuss your issues when they are small, so they don't build up and become monster issues that are much more difficult and time-consuming to resolve.

3. WHY CAN'T MY PARTNER TAKE MY ADVICE ON SOMETHING, INSTEAD OF COMING BACK A FEW DAYS LATER AND ACTING LIKE HE JUST FIGURED IT OUT FOR HIMSELF?

You know the situation: You and your partner are discussing whether to go to the seashore for a holiday, or to a nearby lake. You try to convince your partner that going to the seashore would be a mistake—this time of year, it's crowded with people, and you've heard recently that it's become a hang-out for teenagers—and the lake is quiet, less expensive, and more romantic. Your partner doesn't appear very open to hearing your point of view, and even argues that the seashore would be a change of pace. You know he doesn't want to go to the seashore. You know he agrees with you. But he refuses to give in.

A few days pass, and one evening over dinner your partner turns to you and says, "You know, I've been thinking. I have a feeling the seashore is going to be really crowded this year, with all those kids out of school and everything. I know the lake will be more relaxing. I think we should go to the lake for our vacation, honey." And you sit there in silent disbelief, amazed that your partner doesn't "remember" that you suggested the very same thing a few days earlier.

The answer to this question lies in some of what we've talked about earlier in the book:

▼ **Men need to feel they are right.** In case you haven't noticed, men are very competitive, even with their wives or girlfriends. Somehow, when you come up with an idea, even though a man may agree, he feels "wrong" for having not thought of it first. Giving in and admitting you are right makes some men feel you are smarter than them, something they would never want to acknowledge to themselves.

▼ **Men like to feel they are in charge.** When you suggest a solution to a problem and a man agrees with you, a part of him feels you are now in control, that you are the dominant force in the relationship. This is a very primal instinct in men, something they will deny until they're blue in the face—but we know it's true!

▼ **Men like to feel independent, and to do things by themselves.** This goes back to the little boy trying to break away from his dependence on Mommy, saying, "No, Mommy, let me tie my shoe—I can do it myself." When a man feels you helped him solve a problem he couldn't solve on his own, he may secretly feel emasculated.

The Solution: It's important to realize that men aren't aware that they do this. Your partner doesn't consciously hear your good suggestion and say, "Darn her, why didn't I think of that. Oh well, I'll wait till Tuesday and then pretend I came up with it myself." And if you question him about it, he'll swear he doesn't remember you mentioning it before Tuesday. The best advice I can give you is to discuss this subject with the man in your life, have him read these pages, and see what happens. After all, this isn't a relationship-threatening habit—just an exasperating one!

4. WHY ISN'T MY PARTNER AS EXPRESSIVE AND APPRECIATIVE TOWARD ME AS I AM TOWARD HIM?

Here's the situation: You and your partner have planned a wonderful evening out together—dinner and dancing. You've spent an hour and a half doing your hair, your nails, your make-up, and getting dressed in a new outfit. You walk into the living room to greet your mate and you say, "Here I am, honey. How do I look?" Your partner looks at you for a second and says, "You look nice." Then he walks away to get the car keys.

You stand there feeling awful. "Nice," you think to yourself. "Is that all he can say?" When your mate returns, you tell him you feel a little hurt. "But I said you looked nice," he answers with surprise. "What else do you want me to say?"

"Well, you didn't notice my new dress, or comment on my hair, or anything."

"You know what your problem is?" your partner says, raising his voice. "You're never satisifed—nothing I ever do is good enough for you. You're always telling me I did it wrong." And as you stand there fighting, you feel totally confused and can't even figure out why this is happening.

Here's what's happening: **Men don't notice details the way women do.** Let's recall Chapter 1, when we talked about men's genetic history. Men have always been trained to have broad awareness, and women have been trained to have detail awareness: men scanned the horizon for enemy tribes, while women watched the fire and the children; men thought about how many acres of land they could plow in a day, and what to plant for the next year, while women thought about what to cook for dinner that night; men worried about making enough money to send the kids to college and pay the mortgage, while women worried about whether the kids had any clean underwear for school tomorrow. One kind of awareness isn't better than the other—they're just different ways that men and women have been accustomed to noticing the world around them.

Now you know this already:

How many times have you commented on a friend's furniture after visiting their home with your husband, and had him respond: "Were their couches blue? I didn't notice."

Have you ever asked your partner, "You know my green cotton dress with the white bow—do you think that would look better for your cousin's wedding than the black velvet suit?" and had him look at you blankly as you realize he doesn't even remember the outfits you are talking about.

Most, but not all, men don't notice as much color, shape, texture and detail as women. Women are trained to notice detail. The problem is that:

▼

WOMEN UNCONSCIOUSLY EXPECT MEN TO HAVE THE SAME KIND OF PERCEPTION THAT WE DO

▲

So when you ask your partner, "How do I look?" you expect the same kind of response you would give him if he asked you that question—details, details, details. You know, the kind of response your girlfriends give you when they see you in a new outfit: "Oh, Barbara, is that new? I love it. Turn around, let me see the back. Oh, it's great. That color looks so good on you. You know, it's really a flattering style to your figure. And how did you find earrings to match—they go perfectly. You just look wonderful."

It's not that men don't want to tell you how they feel, or to appreciate you—they just don't put their attention on it, and aren't in the habit of paying attention that specifically. In fact, most men aren't even aware of this problem and will not understand this unless you explain it to them.

The Solution: **Train your partner to notice details.** Point out details to him about how he looks, or what you like about a house you pass by on a Sunday drive, or what you think is so beautiful about a scene in a park:

▼

Male way: **"This is a nice suit."**

Female way: **"What an attractive suit, honey. Look at the subtle colors woven into the material—there's a little red and blue in there. It tapers really nicely in at the waist, too, and really flatters your build. It's made very well—you can tell from how the lapels are sewn."**

▲

▼

Male way: "That's a nice house over there."

Female way: "What a great-looking house. Look at that landscaping—isn't it lovely? And there are so many French windows and doors. I love the way they painted it white with that unusual blue trim. It looks so fresh."

▲

▼

Male way: "Gee, the park sure looks beautiful today."

Female way: "I love being in the park, and just sitting here in the sun. This time of day, everything looks so clear with the sun shining on it. Can you believe how many different shades of green there are in that grove of trees over there? Look how puffy the clouds are— they look like they're about to burst. I feel so peaceful when I'm here."

▲

This trains your partner to begin to notice and comment on details himself.

When your partner compliments you, or admires something, ask him to be more specific. Let's say your partner says, "I like your outfit, honey." Don't just say thank you— ask him what he likes about it. If he says, "I like the color," ask, "Do you like this color better than the blue colors I wear?" In other words, help him train his mind to notice details and express his feelings about them.

Remember: The history of literature proves that men are just as poetic and expressive as women are, but many twentieth-century men need a little practice to stimulate that detail-oriented awareness again.

5. WHY DOES MY PARTNER ALWAYS GET SO ANGRY AND
DEFENSIVE WHEN HE'S UPSET INSTEAD OF TELLING ME
WHAT'S REALLY BOTHERING HIM?

You and your partner are sitting in the den after dinner.
You can tell that something is bothering him. You ask him
what's wrong, and he says, "Nothing."

"Come on, honey," you persist, "I know something is
upsetting you—you can talk to me."

"I said, everything is fine, so quit bugging me," he
responds in an icy tone of voice.

"Well, you don't sound like everything is fine, you sound
really angry," you continue.

"Look, just get off my back," your partner yells. "Why
are you always watching me like a hawk? You're right, now I
am angry—I'm angry at you for being so damn bitchy."

Why is it that sometimes, the only emotion men seem
to be able to show is anger? They react with anger when
they are feeling scared or worried. They react with anger
when they are feeling hurt by something you did. They react
with anger when they're feeling guilty about something. They
may even react with anger if they feel they love and need
you too much.

Let's go back to a man's childhood for the answer. Until
recently, most little boys were taught that they can't show
their vulnerable feelings, like hurt, fear, or need. These are
weak emotions, all right for girls to feel, but not for boys.
Boys whose feelings get hurt, or who cry, or who say they're
scared are ridiculed and called sissies. Boys are rewarded for
being strong and tough and acting "like a man." It's
acceptable to get angry, or get into a fight, but not to break
down and cry.

By suggesting the emotions your partner may not be in
touch with himself, you can help lead him away from his
anger and make it safe for him to express the other, more
vulnerable feelings.

"Honey, I know how upset you must be over Fred's heart attack. He's your best friend, and so close to your own age. I know I always feel frightened when someone I love gets that sick—I hate thinking about losing people I love so much. You must feel so helpless, wanting to do something to make him better, and having to just wait."

Give your partner a lot of positive feedback when he does express even a little of his vulnerability. Remember: Men have received so much negative feedback for being vulnerable—and still do in many parts of our society—that they need all the encouragement and positive reinforcement you can give them. When your partner opens up even a little bit, tell him how much it means to you and how proud you are of him. I'm not talking about being patronizing—I'm suggesting that you give men support for doing something that is quite scary for them.

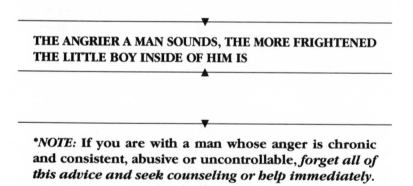

THE ANGRIER A MAN SOUNDS, THE MORE FRIGHTENED THE LITTLE BOY INSIDE OF HIM IS

***NOTE:** If you are with a man whose anger is chronic and consistent, abusive or uncontrollable, forget all of this advice and seek counseling or help immediately.*

The Male-to-Female Dictionary

After reading through this chapter, I'm sure you can see why I started out by saying that men and women speak different languages. To help sum up everything we've discussed, here's a Male-to-Female Dictionary. Just as a French-to-English dictionary takes the French word and

Phrase	Translation
"I don't want to talk about it right now."	"I need some time to figure out how I'm feeling. I'm afraid if I answer now, I might say the wrong thing. I can't think as fast as you can when it comes to finding words to express my emotions."
"Calm down—you're getting too emotional."	"I feel like I'm supposed to fix you, but I don't know how. I feel responsible for your pain. I don't know how to help you."
"Look, this is the way I am. Guys are just raised this way."	"I'm afraid something is wrong with me. I'm afraid I can't change. I don't always understand my own behavior."
"Look, I said I'm sorry. What else do you want me to say?"	"I'm afraid you won't forgive me. I feel like a jerk for hurting you. I'm embarrassed that you had to see me make a mistake."
"Honey, I have to get up really early tomorrow—do you think this is a good idea?" [said in bed at night during foreplay]	"I'm really in the mood for some quick sex, but I'm afraid I'll sound selfish if I ask for it."
"Why are you always making it sound like everything is my fault? What about what you did wrong?"	"I hate admitting that you're right about something. I'm angry at myself for not figuring things out as quickly as you did."

translates it to English, this Male-to-Female Dictionary takes common phrases men use and provides translations of what they really mean in a language women can understand. I've only included a few items from the Male-to-Female Dictionary—I suggest you use these examples to figure out your own translations of your partner's favorite phrases that drive you crazy. You might even want to sit down with the man in your life and ask him to help create the dictionary with you. Of course, don't be surprised if he agrees—but only on the condition that you write him a Female-to-Male Dictionary!

I hope you've found this chapter on communicating with men both enlightening and helpful. You'll need to read it over and over again until this information becomes second nature to you. Please share what you've learned with the men in your life. They'll feel understood and can work together with you on creating loving, effective communication.

8 Helping the Man You Love Open Up

"I know my boyfriend is emotionally shut down. He really doesn't trust love, and he's been hurt pretty badly in the past. He pretends he's not interested in that emotional stuff, as he calls it, and gets really sarcastic when I try to talk with him about how he feels. But I just know that my love will help him change. He's never had anyone love him like that before. *If I love him enough, I know he'll open up."*

I wish I could tell you that this kind of fantasy comes true. I wish I could write this chapter and say, "If you love your man enough, he will open up to you." But I can't, because it isn't true. I know. I've tried it, and it doesn't work.

It's not that your love doesn't make a difference—it does. Sometimes the man opens up a little bit, but not enough to make the relationship work. Sometimes he opens up a lot, but he takes a long time to do it, and by then, you are so

261

angry and used up that you can't receive his love. Sometimes you leave him, and suddenly, the residual effect of your love sinks in and he opens up—only it's too late, because you're gone. No matter how it happens, you end up feeling the same way I did: ripped off; betrayed; hopeless; wondering, If you had just loved him a little more, would it have made a difference. And in the end you're left with a broken heart, the kind women get when we offer a man our love and he turns it away.

▼

THERE IS ONLY ONE WAY TO HELP A MAN OPEN UP: HE HAS TO BE WILLING TO HELP HIMSELF

▲

Your love *can* make a difference in a man's life—it can give him the support, safety and courage he needs to face his inner world of feeling. But all your efforts and discussions and tears won't be enough—he has to make a commitment to his own process of personal growth. He has to want to open up. Only then can you help him.

There's a difference between working together with a man on his emotional growth, and taking on the responsibility of doing it for him.

Many times, when we as women claim we're helping our man open his heart, we'd be much more honest and accurate to admit that we keep trying to pry it open and he keeps slamming it shut. As we saw in Chapter 3, we often fill in the emotional blanks in our relationship with a man, doing all or most of the "rowing." Part of creating healthy relationships for yourself is knowing the difference between the men who really do want your help in opening up, and the men who don't.

Does Your Partner Want to Open Up?

A young couple came to me on the verge of a breakup. The woman complained that, in spite of her efforts, her partner refused to open up emotionally in the way she wanted him to. When I asked her boyfriend to explain his side of the conflict, he answered, *"I didn't ask her to try to fix me."*

▼

ONE OF THE BIGGEST MISTAKES WOMEN MAKE WITH MEN IS DECIDING ON AN AGENDA FOR THE RELATIONSHIP WITHOUT INFORMING THEIR PARTNER

▲

You may think your partner needs to learn to communicate better, or be more vulnerable, or get in touch with more of his emotions. But it's not what you think that counts—it's what *he* thinks. When you decide what direction your relationship will take without consulting your partner, you are not only *not* respecting his rights, you're setting yourself up for major disappointment.

So before you even think about *how* to help your partner open up, you need to ask yourself: **Does my partner *want* to open up?**

What's the best way of determining this? Simple—ask him! Naturally, I'm not suggesting that on your first date with a man, you say, "Hello, my name is Barbara. Tell me something: Are you interested in opening up emotionally?" You should, however, take the following steps.

How to Tell If a Man Wants to Open Up Emotionally

1. Make sure you know what qualities you're looking for in a partner. Write out a compatibility list, such as the one I describe in *How to Make Love All the Time.* Here are some examples from a list:

Likes to talk about feelings;
Has done some personal growth work on himself;
Enjoys being affectionate;
Has a flexible intellect.

2. Discuss the kind of man you want and the kind of relationship you'd like to create with your prospective partner. Be specific, and ask him if his perception of himself matches your wish list.

3. Ask your prospective partner to describe his picture of what he wants a relationship to look like. Be careful—don't put words in his mouth.

4. Think about the information this new person has given you. Observe his behavior for the next few dates to see if he's just all talk or if he really does demonstrate the qualities you're looking for in a man. If he's still looking good, go ahead.

5. As your relationship becomes more serious, and you decide you are "officially" a couple, ask your partner to make a list of the emotional goals he'd like to achieve during the course of your relationship. For instance:

▼ I'd like to learn to ask for help when I'm overwhelmed rather than doing everything myself.

▼ I'd like to feel safe sharing my vulnerable feelings, like fear or hurt, and not just the positive feelings.

▼ I'd like to learn to talk about problems when they are small, rather than avoiding them, telling myself everything's "fine," and waiting until I blow up.

▼ I'd like to learn how to be more sensitive to my partner's needs, so I don't get so caught up in my own life and work that she feels neglected.

Naturally, you should make a list of your own emotional goals as well.

The purpose of this exercise is to make sure the man you love is motivated to open up on his own. By setting his own goals, he's making a commitment to his *own* growth process.

6. Share lists with your partner, and create a plan for achieving each of those goals by making agreements for your relationship. These agreements are like "rules" you both agree to follow in order to achieve your own emotional goals and behave in a way that supports the harmony of the relationship. In the next chapter, I'll teach you how to create a Relationship Rule Book. When your partner makes rules for himself, he's taking responsibility for his own process of opening up.

If you are already in a relationship, you can still use this formula to help your partner focus on his own goals for himself and the two of you, and for you to articulate what you need and want.

Once your partner has made a concrete commitment to work on opening up emotionally, you can support and encourage him with confidence, knowing he wants to help himself, and that you are working as a team.

I can't emphasize strongly enough how important the above information is. Believe me, I know from personal experience how tempting it will be to read this, think to yourself, "These are good suggestions," and then ignore them completely by making a man into a "project" and trying to "fix" him when he hasn't committed to fixing himself.

HOW TO TELL WHEN A MAN ISN'T GOING TO OPEN UP

There's a point in a relationship where you want to give your partner the benefit of the doubt, and do everything you can to be patient, and make him feel safe to go through his own process. And unfortunately, there's a point in some relationships where you need to admit to yourself that your partner just isn't going to change, and that no matter how much you are willing to help, it's not doing any good.

Here are some warning signs to watch out for.

You Can't Help a Man When:

1 You're doing more for him than he's doing for himself.

2 He has a negative, hopeless attitude toward life. ("Nothing ever works out for me. Life is unfair.")

3 He always blames others for his problems and refuses to take responsibility for his situation.

4 He has destructive addictions he refuses to face and conquer: drugs, alcohol, food, or gambling.

5 He has a chronic need to be in control and therefore creates constant power struggles with you over everything.

6 He has a lot of guilt, blame, and low self-esteem due to unresolved incidents from his past. (He left his wife and kids and never forgave himself. He hasn't spoken to his father in twenty years.)

7 He makes excuses for his behavior, claiming, "This is just the way I am."

8 He refuses to participate in seeking help for himself and the relationship, through counseling, seminars, or reading books.

9 He tells you he doesn't *want* to open up!

Obviously, all men do some of the things on this list once in a while. But if these warning signs look all too familiar to you, please don't ignore them. Confront your partner with your fears seek outside help, and go back and read Chapter 3 about how to stop filling in the emotional blanks. Remember: It takes two involved, committed people to make a relationship work.

SOME OTHER WAYS TO HELP THE MAN YOU LOVE

▼ **Encourage your partner to develop more quality male friends.** Most men have a difficult time creating close male friendships. Their training to be competitive and mistrustful of one another makes real emotional bonding difficult. But men need friendships with other men—it gives them an outlet for parts of themselves they can't fully share with women. Even though your picture of friendship may be different from what you see your partner doing with another man, support him anyway. Men have their own language and own ways of being intimate. Your husband might spend three hours with a buddy talking about his new stereo system, and tell you that that filled his need for closeness. You might think "Is he kidding?" He's not. Remember: Men can't fathom why women like to go shopping together either!

▼ **Suggest that your partner become involved in men's support groups or rap groups.** Men tend to isolate themselves not only from women, but from the society of other men as a whole. There are more and more "male only" groups in every city, led by male therapists or health professionals. Although the idea of spending a few hours with a group of men talking about issues and emotions might not appeal to your partner at first, he'll find the experience to be a powerful affirmation of his own thoughts and feelings, and a source of tremendous support.

▼ **Buy your partner books written by men about men.** There is so much publicity about women's self-help books that the books written for men are sometimes lost in the crush. There are some excellent books that have been published in the last few years that explain more about the male experience from a man's point of view. Go to a bookstore and browse through the psychology section. Choose some books you think your partner will find interesting, and give them to him as a gift. Then, after he's done reading them, ask him what he thought about the information, what he learned, and what parts he would like you read so you can understand him better.

Here are a few books I recommend: *Secrets Men Keep* by Ken Druck; *In a Man's World* by Perry Garfinckle; *Male Sexuality* by Bernie Zilbergeld; *Why Can't Men Open Up* by Steven Naifeh and Gregory White Smith; and *The Male Midlife Crisis* by Nancy Mayer.

▼ **Take your partner to a personal-growth seminar.** I can tell you from my own experience teaching seminars for the past ten years that men can make tremendous emotional breakthroughs in the right workshop setting. Most fairly large cities have a variety of courses available through universities, churches, or synagogues, or private organizations such as the Making Love Work seminars I teach. If you can't find information on these activities, go to a local health store, pick up one of the free personal-growth newspapers distributed in most regions of the country, and read through the advertisements of seminars in your city or nearby. Don't attend a seminar with the intention of fixing your partner—be there for yourself.

How to Tell If You're Helping Too Much

Here's a chart I've created to aid you in telling the difference between helping a man you love and going overboard. The left column lists helping behaviors that are okay; the right column lists reactions that are too extreme.

O.K. Help	Too Much
Let him know you want to talk to him, and don't pressure him if it's not the right time.	Let him always control when you talk about problems.
Give him time to come up with a response when you ask his opinion or need a commitment from him on something.	Keep pestering him about it when he never comes back with his answer.
Give him lots of acknowledgment and praise so he feels safe and that he's doing it "right."	You don't receive an equal amount of acknowledgment and praise back.
Give him a chance to make his own mistakes without mothering him.	Let his irresponsibility and laziness constantly interfere with your life.
Set a loving example by being affectionate, planning surprises, or giving cards and gifts.	Keep filling in the emotional blanks in the relationship—you're rowing the boat and he's a passenger.
Help him get in touch with his feelings by leading him through the Emotional Map and duplicating the emotions inside of him.	Figure out his feelings for him—he counts on you to "pull him out."
Avoid making him feel "wrong" by being overly critical or full of blame when he makes mistakes.	You never give him negative feedback because you feel he can't handle hearing it.
Understand the importance of his work and support him in this area.	Put up with him being a workaholic, using his job to avoid himself and the relationship.
Be careful not to treat your partner like an incompetent child.	Acknowledge him only as an adult and never play with the little boy inside him.
Be sensitive to his moods and his need to feel loved and accepted.	Walk around on eggshells, afraid of upsetting him.

In a man's struggle to open up, he needs a woman's help. Sometimes I think that women are emotional midwives, helping men give birth to the feelings and sensitivity that exist within them. But no matter how much you love a man, you can't get him to open up on your own.

▼

WHEN YOU FIND A MAN WHO IS COMMITTED TO HIS OWN PROCESS OF BECOMING A LOVING, GIVING HUMAN BEING, YOUR RELATIONSHIP WILL MOVE BEYOND A POWER STRUGGLE TO COOPERATION

▲

There's nothing more frustrating than trying to get through to a man you love who just won't push aside his emotional barriers and let you into his heart. And there's nothing more wonderful than loving a man who passionately and courageously throws himself into his relationship with you, trusting that your love will help him grow into the sensitive and powerful man he knows he can be.

9 Becoming the Powerful Woman You Were Meant to Be

True intimacy with another human being can be experienced only when you have found true peace within yourself.

—Angela L. Wozniak

The journey from the woman you've been to the woman you dream of becoming is not always an easy one. It takes a lot of time and effort to change from frightened to courageous, from self-sacrificing to self-supporting, from powerless to powerful. I wrote this book as a manual not just for you to better understand men, but for you to better understand yourself as a woman.

So many times throughout these pages, we've seen that in our efforts to transform the men in our lives, we often forget about transforming ourselves. This is one of the most disguised and damaging ways we as women give our power away. We neglect our own process of personal growth, and thereby postpone our discovery of the magnificent feminine spirit that lives within each of us.

271

Steps You Can Take to Become a More Powerful Woman

POWER TIP **1** ———————————————————

Do All the Exercises in This Book.

Throughout this book I've included many exercises, checklists, and dos and don'ts to help you be a more powerful woman and get along better with the men in your life. *Please use these tools and techniques.* They really work! I've shared them with thousands of women, and apply them daily in my own life. You don't have to make every list and try every new suggestion at once. You might try going through the book a few pages at a time and working with the principles and techniques on those pages.

Note: Pay special attention to the exercises in Chapter 2, "The Six Biggest Mistakes Women Make with Men," and Chapter 3, "Filling in the Emotional Blanks." These will help you uncover your negative behavior patterns that keep you from having fulfilling relationships.

POWER TIP **2** ———————————————————

Make a Relationship Mistake List and a Relationship Rule Book.

The Relationship Mistake List is a more personalized version of the six biggest mistakes women make with men; the twenty sexual turn-offs, the communication mistakes, and the other lists of women's behavioral habits we've explored in the book. Here's how to do it:

STEP 1: MAKE A RELATIONSHIP MISTAKE LIST

Sit down and think back over all of your relationships with men, both personal and professional. Write down everything you can see that you did wrong in relating to those men, based on your new understanding from this book. For instance:

Sample Relationship Mistake List

1. I try to impress men I'm interested in by talking a lot about myself. I'm so worried about how I look to them that I never ask myself how they look to me.
2. I hold in my negative feelings toward my partner because I don't want to rock the boat or get him upset, and then end up slowly turning off to him inside.
3. I talk too much about my ex-husband and how angry I still am at him, and end up turning off my partner.
4. When I'm unhappy with how I'm being treated, I pout or act like a little girl, rather than asking directly for what I want or sticking up for myself.
5. I don't give the man in my life a chance to do romantic things for me since I'm always doing them first.
6. I give too much advice to the man I love, acting like his mother, and scolding him when he doesn't live up to my expectations.

Your Relationship Mistake List should be quite long, with at least thirty or more items. To help you focus in on your mistakes, read through the book, and whenever you notice a pattern that fits you, write it down. Put aside the first draft of your list for a few days, and you'll notice that you'll remember other mistakes or notice yourself making them. Add these to the list.

STEP 2: MAKE A RELATIONSHIP RULE BOOK

Take each mistake one by one, and write a rule for yourself that will help you avoid making that mistake again. For instance:

Sample Relationship Rule Book

Rule #1

When I find myself trying to impress a man I like by talking so much about myself that I'm not asking him any questions, I'll stop performing and focus on whether he is right for me.

Rule #2

I'll express my negative feelings as soon as I become aware of them, rather than waiting until they build up—even if it means upsetting my partner.

Rule #3

I'll work on healing my relationship with my ex-husband by looking at how I set myself up to be hurt, and I won't talk about him as if I'm the victim and he's the villain.

Rule #4

When my feelings are hurt, I'll tell my partner how I'm feeling rather than pouting, getting even, pretending I don't care or acting like a little girl.

Rule #5

When I find myself filling in the blanks, I'll stop and ask myself if my partner has given much back to me lately. If he hasn't, I'll ask him for what I need rather than making things better myself.

Rule #6

When I find myself giving unsolicited advice or treating my partner like a little boy, I'll stop, take a deep breath, and let him figure it out on his own, unless he asks for help.

Be sure to make a rule for each mistake on your list. Of course, you can add new rules each time you notice yourself making another mistake.

STEP 3: MAKE SEVERAL COPIES OF YOUR RULE BOOK AND READ THEM FREQUENTLY.

The more familiar you become with your rule book, the less frequently you'll make those same old mistakes. I suggest you make several copies of your Relationship Rule Book. Carry one copy with you at all times, in your wallet; keep one copy by your bed and read it first thing in the morning; tack one copy on the refrigerator (unless you don't want your partner to see it).

Read your rule book frequently, until you practically have those new rules memorized.

STEP 4: SHARE YOUR RULE BOOK WITH YOUR PARTNER AND/OR SOME FRIENDS TO ENLIST THEIR SUPPORT FOR YOUR NEW COMMITMENTS.

If you really are serious about making a change, share your rule book with your partner. He'll appreciate your commitment and might even have some rules of his own to suggest. Ask him to "bust" you when he notices that you're breaking one of your rules. You can also use your girlfriends as a support system for helping you stick to your new rules.

STEP 5: ASK YOUR PARTNER TO MAKE HIS OWN MISTAKE LIST AND RULE BOOK.

If you and your partner are going to work as a team to create a magnificent relationship, you're both going to need to make a list and a rule book. Once you've completed yours, your partner hopefully will be encouraged to do the same.

Making a Relationship Rule Book for yourself is one of the most powerful steps you can take toward actually changing your behavior. Each time you find yourself about to make one of those old mistakes, you can catch yourself, remember the new rule, and have a new direction to go in.

POWER TIP 3

Create a Support System of Women in Your Life.

Women often ignore one of their greatest resources for inspiration and support—other women. When we view other women as the competition, potential threats that might take our man away, we really are ripping ourselves off. Women can help each other grow in a way that no man ever can. We can feel each other's pain as if it is our own; we can rejoice in each other's strength and celebrate each other's victories as if we ourselves had accomplished them. We are, after all, different facets of the same jewel, the female soul.

▼

THE MORE LOVE AND SUPPORT YOU RECEIVE FROM FEMALE FRIENDS IN YOUR LIFE, THE LESS DEPENDENT YOU WILL BE ON A MAN TO FULFILL ALL OF YOUR NEEDS

▲

There is a quality of attention and support you can only receive from other women, and expecting it from men will only disappoint you. We might as well face the fact: *Men will never be women.* And I believe that the more you allow women to fill your needs for a certain kind of love and relating, the more you can gratefully accept and appreciate what a man can give you as a man.

Here are some suggestions:

▼ **Join a women's support group, or form your own.** Create a support group of women who are interested in transforming themselves and their relationships with men. You might start out by meeting once a month, and discussing some of the things you learned in this book and some of the habits you're trying to change. One idea would be to talk about one section or concept from the book each week or month. I suggest you share your Mistake Lists and Rule Books with each other so you don't feel as if you're the only one who has such a long list, and encourage each other to follow those new, healthier behavior patterns. Working with other women will keep you inspired and motivated to put these new principles into practice.

▼ **Become Power Buddies with another woman.** A Power Buddy is someone who agrees to be your partner while you both go through a process of intense personal transformation. You and a female friend sit down together and create emotional goals for yourself, share your mistake lists and rule books, and commit yourselves to supporting one another in every way you can. For instance, when you find yourself feeling like victim and giving your power away to your partner, you call your Power Buddy and ask for a pep talk. Even when you become confused, your Power Buddy will hopefully be clear and can guide you back to a more centered, powerful place.

POWER TIP 4 ─────────────────

Maintain Your Dignity.

In Part I of this book, we talked about what it meant for you as a woman to maintain your dignity. I wanted to remind you about this phrase once more, because I think it is contains such a powerful message. Spend some time thinking about what it means for you to maintain your dignity. Maybe it means not having sex with someone until he's made some form of commitment to your relationship. Maybe it's never tolerating being yelled at or threatened by your partner. Maybe it's not allowing yourself to be talked out of your feelings. Use this phrase as your new "mantra." Meditate on it when you're feeling upset; write it down and post it in places where you'll read it frequently.

Are We Really That Different After All?

While writing this book, I shared the finished chapters with some very close friends. Their reactions were very interesting. All the women said they could relate to all my secrets about men, and felt I was talking to them as well. All of the men admitted that they made many of the mistakes I attributed to women. "You're beginning to get the picture," I'd respond with a smile. "Beneath all our conditioning, men and women aren't that different after all."

▼

MEN AND WOMEN ALL WANT THE SAME THINGS—TO FEEL WORTHWHILE, TO FEEL GOOD ABOUT THEMSELVES, AND TO BE LOVED

▲

My purpose in writing about men and women as I did was *not* to create more distance and separation between the sexes, but to build a bridge of understanding between us.

I'm sure that as you read through the book, you noticed that you were guilty of some of the characteristics I attributed to men, and that your partner sometimes fit the female examples more than the male ones. Naturally, everything I've presented won't apply perfectly to you or to the man in your life. Don't use that as an excuse to invalidate the information that does apply to you! And remember—you can apply what you've learned with all the men in your life: your brothers, your father, your friends, your coworkers, your boss.

THE BIRTH OF A BOOK

As I sit at my computer, waiting for the last sentences of my book to pour out of me, I think of my best friend Jamie, who is about to have a baby any minute now. Jamie and I have a joke that she can't go into labor until I finish this book, and since she's due today, I've spent the morning furiously typing, hoping the phone doesn't ring before my final words touch the page.

In more ways than I can describe, writing this book has been a process of giving birth for me, and I've never been more aware of it than I am right now, laboring over the final moments, reaching deep within for the strength to push the last piece of myself out. I once heard someone say that "Woman is the vehicle of life." We give forth life from our own bodies; we instill life in others with our love. We celebrate the miracle of life in the process of our own perpetual rebirth.

Like Jamie's baby, this book was conceived in love. It is the love I feel for the men in my life who have taught me, sometimes through joy and sometimes through sorrow, about the singular beauty of the male spirit. They have helped me find the words to describe their mysterious silences, and they remind me, with each new relationship, that love is always worth it, no matter what the outcome.

It is the love I feel for women; for my mother, for my grandmothers, for my friends, for every woman who's reached out to me over the radio or trusted me in a seminar, or who I've held in my arms while she wept frightened tears, all of whom taught me that I am not alone in my search for a gentle world.

And most of all, it is the love I feel for the gift of love itself—that we can feel it so deeply for so many people in such different ways; that even when we say good-bye, we may lose a person, but we never lose the love; that, like the miracles of life, love renews itself over and over again. Love has been my greatest source of pain as well as my greatest source of peace, and therefore, my most patient and powerful teacher.

Giving birth to this book has not been easy for me. It has forced me to face my own emptinesses and my own blind spots more than anything I have ever done before. It has put me back in touch with dreams of how I want to be loved that I had forgotten. But most of all it has made me appreciate my own emotional courage—the courage to continue believing in love, even when loving has broken my heart, the courage to begin again and again.

So Jamie's ready to deliver her baby, and I'm ready to deliver this book to my publisher. Like a child, it will now have a life of its own, separate from me, yet always connected. And just as a piece of every mother's heart goes with her child, a piece of my heart is going with this book to you.

I hope that in some small way I've helped to bring more harmony and happiness into your life, and I pray that your own special dreams of love come true.

FOR MORE INFORMATION

Secrets About Men Every Woman Should Know was inspired by the experiences of the thousands of people who have undergone a powerful emotional transformation after attending Dr. Barbara De Angelis's **Making Love Work seminar.** Dr. De Angelis teaches her seminar once a month in Los Angeles. The seminar takes place over a weekend, and is open to singles, couples, and families interested in creating more love in their lives.

Dr. De Angelis is available for lectures, conferences, workshops, and speaking engagements throughout the country, and enjoys inspiring her audiences on the topics of love, relationships, success, and personal motivation.

To contact Dr. De Angelis
please write or call:

Dr. Barbara De Angelis
1904 Centinela Avenue
Los Angeles, CA 90025
(213) 820-6600

1-800-422-9993

The Phone Number That Can Change Your Life!

SECRETS ABOUT MEN EVERY WOMAN SHOULD KNOW

——————— T H E V I D E O ———————

Starring Dr. Barbara De Angelis

- ❏ Your very own private seminar!
- ❏ A full 80 minutes in length!
- ❏ Hear other women share their secrets and concerns!
- ❏ Watch men reveal their fears, desires, and intimate feelings that will give you the inside track!

YES! I WANT THE "SECRETS"!

Please send me my own VHS video today for $39.95 plus $3.50 postage & handling. (California residents add 6.5% tax.)

Make orders payable to:
100% Productions, Ltd.
5959 Triumph Street
Commerce, CA 90040-1688

**ONLY $39.**^{95}
plus $3.50 postage
OR
ORDER BY PHONE!
1-800-422-9993

NAME: _____ Phone: _____

ADDRESS: _____

City: _____ State: _____ Zip: _____

VISA ___ MASTERCARD ___ AMEX ___ CHECK ___ Acct.#: _____

Exp. Date: _____ Signature _____

Please allow 3–4 weeks for delivery

©1989 Barbara De Angelis Corp. & David Sams Industries—A 100% Production

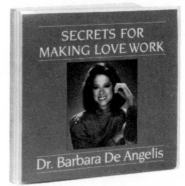